MW00475133

PRESENTED TO

_____

BY

_____

DATE

_____

THE TONGUE

A Creative Force

THE TONGUE

a creative force

CHARLES CAPPS

Published by Harrison House Publishers
Shippensburg, PA 17257

ISBN 13: 978-1-6803-1799-2

For Worldwide Distribution, Printed in the U.S.A.

1 2 3 4 5 6 7 8 / 26 25 24 23 22

"If any man among you seem to be religious, and bridleth not his tongue, but deceiveth his own heart, this man's religion is vain."

James 1:26

"Even so the tongue is a little member, and boasteth great things. Behold, how great a matter a little fire kindleth! And the tongue is a fire, a world of iniquity: so is the tongue among our members, that it defileth the whole body, and setteth on fire the course of nature: and it is set on fire of hell...But the tongue can no man tame; it is an unruly evil, full of deadly poison."

James 3:5-6,8

CONTENTS

CHAPTER 1

WORDS

God's Word that is conceived in your heart, then formed by the tongue, and spoken out of your own mouth, becomes a spiritual force releasing the ability of God within you.

That's why Paul said, **"I can do all things through Christ which strengtheneth me"** (Phil. 4:13). *His heart (spirit) had received God's Word.* It was not Paul's ability that made him say that, but the ability of God formed in him by the Word, and out of the abundance of his heart his mouth spoke.

Those that say they can and those that say they can't are both right. Words are the most powerful thing in the universe. We read in John 1:1, **"In the beginning was the**

Word, and the Word was with God, and the Word was God." We must learn to use our words more effectively. *The words you speak will either put you over or hold you in bondage.* Today, many Christian people have been taken captive by their own words. By the prayer of their own mouth they have been set in a position where they cannot receive from God. We have all done it at one time or another. We have used our tongue to form the very words that defeat us. We have even prayed contrary to the Word of God. *We have prayed defeat and received it. We have prayed the problem and it became greater. Even prayer produces after its kind.* In Mark 11:24 the Word says, **"...What things soever ye DESIRE when ye pray, BELIEVE that ye receive them, and ye shall have them."** Jesus has set forth a great truth about spiritual law. *GOD'S WORD is spiritual law.* It functions just as sure as any natural law.

We have learned how to work with natural law. In dealing with the natural law that governs electricity, we have learned that if we work with that law by obeying and enforcing it, that electrical force will work for us. But if we continually violate that law that governs or controls electricity, we will get in a *"heap of trouble."* As long as we enforce the law that controls electrical forces, it will produce energy to give us light, heat our home, cook our meals, and wash our clothes; and yet it will produce no harm to us. It is very useful and safe, when we understand and apply the law by which it is controlled. However, this same force can burn, kill, and destroy, if the law that governs electricity is not enforced.

So are the words that come forth out of your mouth. They will work *for you* to put you *over in life, IF you control those words* and bring them into obedience to spiritual law, which is *THE WORD OF GOD.* Words governed by spiritual law become spiritual forces working for you. *Idle words work against you.*

THE SPIRIT WORLD IS CONTROLLED BY THE WORD OF GOD.

THE NATURAL WORLD IS TO BE CONTROLLED BY MAN SPEAKING GOD'S WORDS.

THE SPOKEN WORD OF GOD IS CREATIVE POWER.

Therefore, even the words of our prayers should be chosen carefully and spoken accurately. We have often prayed, "Lord I have prayed and it's not working out. The devil has defeated me." But the Word said, "What things soever you desire when you pray, believe you receive...." Defeat is not what you desire, *so don't pray it or say it.* You can see how the wrong choice of words can cause even your prayers to work against you. You have prayed, "Lord, I've got this problem and it's getting worse."

Now let's compare this prayer with the Word of God. First, you have prayed the problem and not the answer. The Word said pray the things you desire. You desire the answer. Second, you have released faith in the ability of the enemy. To make it worse, you established the words of the devil that prayer doesn't work and things are getting worse. You are *walking by sight* and not by *faith.* You have denied the Word of God. You have done it because of the lack of knowledge. In Hosea 4:6 God said, **"My people are destroyed** (cut off) **for lack of knowledge...."** Lack of knowledge has caused men to be destroyed and lives to suffer needless loss.

A few years ago I came upon the scene of an accident. A car had gone out of control and cut off a power pole. The high line wire was hanging about three feet above the ground. Many people had stopped and gotten out of their cars. They were standing no more than three feet away from that live wire, thinking that it was insulated, or that the power was *cut off.* But this was not true; the wire was *"live"* with over 17,000 volts of electricity. I watched from my car, a safe distance away, as the ambulance attendants carried a woman on a stretcher up the highway embankment. As they crawled under the power line one of them got too close, and the electrical current *arced* to his body like a lightning bolt. He died instantly and the other attendant was critically injured.

He violated the natural law that governs electricity. No doubt he did it in ignorance, yet it was fatal.

Lack of knowledge did not stop the electrical force. It continued to work; it was the same force that cooked his meals, heated his house, and washed his clothes. It was created to work for him to make life more enjoyable. The very reason for its existence was to supply his needs, but when he violated the law that controlled that force, it destroyed him.

SPIRITUAL LAW IS FOR YOUR GOOD. It is to produce the things you need and desire. But, speaking and praying contrary to the Word of God (spiritual law) will be just as disastrous as violating the law of electricity. *We have prayed in all manner of prayer that the Bible doesn't teach.* We have prayed to Jesus, and that is an unscriptural way to pray. *Words are important. Begin now to become WORD CONSCIOUS. Words are like little seeds that produce according to the Word of God. God's Word will produce after His kind.* **"A good man out of the good treasure of the heart bringeth forth good things: and an evil man out of the evil treasure bringeth forth evil things"** (Matt. 12:35).

Jesus said, "And in that day ye shall ask me nothing. Verily, verily, I say unto you, Whatsoever ye shall ask the Father in my name, he will give it you. Hitherto have ye asked nothing in my name: *ask, and ye shall receive, that your joy may be full"* (John 16:23,24).

PRAYER IS YOUR LEGAL RIGHT TO USE FAITH-FILLED WORDS TO BRING GOD ON THE SCENE IN YOUR BEHALF, or for another that your JOY MAY BE FULL.

It is the Word abiding in you that causes faith to be present in your words. "If ye abide in me, and my words abide in you, ye shall ask what ye will, and it shall be done unto you. Herein is my Father glorified, that ye bear much fruit; so shall ye be my disciples" (John 15:7,8). Notice it glorifies the Father when you get your prayer answered and your needs met. Verse 11 says, "These things have I spoken unto you, that my joy might remain in you, and that your joy might be full." Your joy can be full if the Word of Mark 11:24 abides in you, "...*When you pray believe...*"

FAITH WILL MAKE PRAYER WORK.

PRAYER WON'T WORK WITHOUT FAITH. FAITH WILL WORK WITHOUT PRAYER. Prayer is one of the means of releasing faith, so if we will line ourselves up with the Word of God and release our faith when we pray, we will see the power of God come alive in our lives.

God's Word is just as powerful today as it was the day He spoke it. Not one bit of power has left God's Word. God's Creative Power® is still in His Word, just as it was when He stood there, in the beginning of time, and said, "Light—be," and light was.

This is the thing I want you to see. *YOU CAN SPEAK GOD'S WORDS AFTER HIM AND THEY WILL*

WORK FOR YOU. But, they must be formed in your spirit. They must become a part of you. *They must abide in you continually.*

THE BEGINNING WORDS

In Genesis 1, it says **"...God created the heavens and earth...."** What did He use to create the heavens and the earth?

Hebrews 11:3 says, "Through faith we understand that the worlds were framed by the word of God, so that things which are seen were not made of things which do appear." The world was not made out of things you can see. *You can't see spoken words nor can you see faith with the physical eye. The words that God spoke out of His mouth framed this universe, set it in motion,* and it stands today in obedience to the words that God spoke. He said, "...Let there be a firmament in the midst of the waters, and let it divide the waters from the waters" (Gen. 1:6). It came into being and divided the waters from the land, and it's still divided from the land today.

The universe is still obeying His command — the Words that God spoke. Because God said it and let it stay said. He didn't back up and say maybe it will, or I hope so. No, He said it by the Word of His mouth and all hell stood up and took notice.

I really believe that millions of years took place between Genesis, chapter one, verse one, when God created the earth, and verse two, where He said the earth was void and without form. Because why would God create an earth without form and void? You see, what went wrong from the beginning was that Satan had come in to destroy the work of God on the earth, and now, there was darkness on the face of the earth. THEN GOD SAID, **"Let there be light."** *It was the creative power that flowed out of God's mouth that turned the universe into light and caused every creation to come into being.*

In Genesis 1:26 we read, "And God said, Let us make man in our image, after our likeness: and let them have dominion over the fish of the sea, and over the fowl of the air, and over the cattle, and over all the earth, and over every creeping thing that creepeth upon the earth." Then God delegated the power to man to dominate this earth.

He created Adam, then He put that authority in Adam, and He said, "now you dominate the earth."

So, Adam was the ruler of the earth.

Then, there came that Snake in the garden. The Snake said to Eve, "You'll not surely die, if you eat of that fruit. God knows you'll be like Him if you eat of that fruit. You'll be wise like God."

Eve ate of the forbidden fruit, and I guess she talked Adam into it, because the Word says, **"And Adam was not deceived, but the woman being deceived was in the transgression"** (1 Tim. 2:14).

Well, Adam ate of the fruit and turned that power and authority over to the enemy; then Satan became the god of this world. "In whom the god of this world hath blinded the minds of them which believe not, lest the light of the glorious gospel of Christ, who is the image of God, should shine unto them" (2 Cor. 4:4).

But Jesus Christ came and got that power back for us. Jesus, God's Word, came and took flesh upon Himself.

Have you wondered how God did that?

Some theologians say it can't be done; a virgin can't bear a child; it's impossible.

We have the Word of God which tells us in Luke 1:37, "For with God nothing shall be impossible." The Concordant literal New Testament says, "It will not be impossible with God to fulfill His every declaration."

Whatever God says, He will perform. If you will notice throughout the Bible, God never did do anything that He didn't say first. He said it, then He did it. The power to do it was in the WORD.

The Bible tells us that "(He is) upholding all things by the Word of His power..." (Heb. 1:3).

It didn't say by the *power of His Word; it said BY THE WORD OF HIS POWER*. The Holy Spirit put that in the exactness — the way He wanted. THE WORD OF HIS POWER.

If He had said the power of His Word, that would have meant that there is some power in God's Word, but not ALL POWER. In other words, that's where *His power is, IN THE WORD,* in what He says.

It's not impossible for God to perform His every declaration. He can declare and do exactly what HE SAYS HE'S GOING TO DO! And we find that God created man with the ability to operate in the same kind of faith.

Control those words that come forth out of your mouth and bring them into obedience to the WORD OF GOD, which is God's spiritual law.

CHAPTER 2

CREATIVE POWER IN YOU

Man was created in the image of God and His likeness. There was creative power that flowed out of the mouth of God, and you were created in the image of God. Then, according to the Scriptures and what Jesus said, you have the same ability dwelling or residing on the inside of you.

Adam gave man's authority over to Satan. Jesus got that authority back. He was born of a virgin.

The way He was born of a virgin was the way that God created the universe. God said it will be done. And it is not impossible for God to perform His every declaration.

When He found a woman who agreed with Him, it could be done, "Then said Mary unto the angel, How shall this be, seeing I know not a man?" (Luke 1:34).

She didn't doubt it could be done. She just asked, "How?" and He said, "...the Holy Ghost shall come upon thee, and the power of the Highest shall overshadow thee..." (Luke 1:35).

In verse 38 Mary said, "...be it done unto me according to thy word...."

She agreed with the WORD, establishing that fact upon the earth, and it came into being.

Now is it so unreasonable to believe that?

God said in His Word that we are **"...born again, not of corruptible seed, but of incorruptible, by the word of God, which liveth and abideth for ever"** (1 Peter 1:23). *The Word of God implanted into your spirit caused you to become a new creation that never existed before, born again of the Spirit of the living God.*

The re-birth of the human spirit took place because the WORD OF GOD LODGED IN YOUR SPIRIT. It caused you to act upon THE WORD, and you were born again. You became a new creation. You were once a sinner, but now YOU'RE BORN AGAIN, THE RIGHTEOUS-NESS OF GOD fully able to stand in the presence of the Father in holy boldness and say, "Father, I come to You in the Name of Your Son, Jesus, without fear of condemnation because I am the righteousness of God in Christ," not a poor sinner, crawling around in the dust, begging and pleading, "Dear Lord, help me please," as some songs say. No, we are the righteousness of God, joint-heirs with Jesus Christ!

That WORD, planted in your spirit, caused you to become a new creation, because the Word of God declared it.

THE WORD MADE FLESH

Now, I want you to see how God caused a virgin to conceive and bear a child. The virgin said, **"be it done unto me according to your Word."**

The Bible says, **"And the Word was made flesh, and dwelt among us..."** (John 1:14). Now the Word was in the beginning with God. The Word came unto Mary and said, *"It will be so."*

Mary said, "I receive it, be it done unto me according to your Word." She first received the Word into her spirit (heart) then it was *manifest in her physical body.* THE WORD OF GOD was implanted into her womb, it was the embryo, the seed, and it took upon itself flesh, just as the living Word of God placed in your spirit took upon itself new creation — life. The Word of God literally formed within her womb and took flesh upon it. The Word of God became alive, living, walking, and talking on this earth. He came here to destroy the work of the devil that was done in Adam.

The work that was done in Adam was destroying the creation of God and the ability of God to work through man.

When Jesus came He took the authority back, and He delegated it back to man, to the believer.

Jesus stood on the mountain before He ascended and said, **"...All power is given unto me in heaven and in earth"** (Matt. 28:18). *He had it ALL.* Then He turned to the believers and said, **"...these signs shall follow them** that believe; In my name shall they cast out devils; they shall speak with new tongues; ...they shall lay hands on the sick, and they shall recover" (Mark 16:17,18).

Jesus is saying, "Now, you go in my name. You cast out demons. You speak with new tongues. You lay hands on the sick and they WILL recover." Now you see God's power, God's authority, delegated back to man. So man is not restored to his original state, (which he was); he is in better shape than he has ever been! Thank God! The born-again man is a joint-heir with Jesus. PRAISE THE NAME OF THE LORD! If Jesus is the righteousness of God, then you are the righteousness of God in Christ.

We need to quit praying and saying, "Lord, I'm unworthy."

Thank God — if Jesus is not unworthy, you're not unworthy. You have a right to stand in the throne room of God.

We've been beaten down, and the devil has just trampled us in the dust because of a sense of unworthiness. I'll tell you, when this WORD gets in your spirit, you'll never be the same. *Lay hold on this Word, rise up and enter into it.*

The enemy knows there is power in your words. That is why he tries so desperately to get you to confess doubt, fear, and unbelief. You see, confessing that you are unworthy after being born again is contrary to the Word. You were unworthy, but that old man died with Christ. You are now a new creation in Christ.

Anyone in Christ cannot be unworthy. The Word says "Therefore if any man be in Christ, he is a new creature: old things are passed away; behold, all things are become new. And all things are of God, who hath reconciled us to himself by Jesus Christ, and hath given to us the ministry of reconciliation; To wit, that God was in Christ, reconciling the world unto himself, not imputing their trespasses unto them; and hath committed unto us the word of reconciliation. Now then we are ambassadors for Christ, as though God did beseech you by us: we pray you in Christ's stead, be ye reconciled to God. For he hath made him to be sin for us, who knew no sin; that we might be made the *righteousness of God in him*" (2 Cor. 5:17-21).

FAITH-FILLED WORDS

Now let's see what Jesus had to say about faith-filled words. I want you to see how He used His words and how they produced for Him. In Mark chapter 11, vs. 11-14, we read, **"And Jesus entered into Jerusalem, and into the temple: and when he had looked round about upon all things, and now the eventide was come, he went out unto Bethany with the twelve. And on the morrow, when they were come from Bethany, he was hungry: And seeing a fig tree afar off having leaves, he came, if haply he might find any thing thereon: and when he came to it, he found nothing but leaves; for the time of figs was not yet. And Jesus answered and said unto it, *No man eat fruit of thee hereafter for ever. And his disciples heard it.*"**

Now Jesus had gone to the fig tree to get some figs and found none. And He said, "No man eat fruit of thee hereafter forever," and He just walked off. When they came back that way the next day, verse 21 says the disciples called Jesus' attention to the fig tree. They said (I'll paraphrase), "The leaves are withered; that thing died from the roots. Did You notice that, Jesus? The tree You cursed."

I always wondered why Jesus *"cussed"* the fig tree. I thought He "cussed" it when I was a little child, but you see, the word *"curse"* means that Jesus spoke *negativism* to it. I want you to notice the words that the Bible uses. It says He put a curse on the fig tree.

Now, we, as believers, have put curses on people by the words of our mouth. I've heard people do it. Someone would come and get saved in the service.

They would say, "Oh, I know them. They get saved every time we have a revival. You just watch, they'll go away and in three weeks, they'll be right back in sin."

And sure enough, they were back in sin. They thought that was a prophetic utterance, but it wasn't; it was a curse.

And they said, "See, I told you so."

They were part of the problem. The words of their mouth worked against that person. Instead of putting faith-filled words there by saying, "God's power is enough to keep them; God's power is enough to hold them; God's power will deliver them, and they'll not fall; I believe they'll stand."

They have been deceived by the evil one to tear down what God was trying to build by the words of their own mouth.

THE GOD KIND OF FAITH

I want you to notice that Jesus knew there was power in His words. *When He spoke to the fig tree, it withered and died.* Now notice, in verse 22 He said, **"Have faith in God,"** or have the GOD KIND OF FAITH. Then in verse 23, Jesus stopped long enough to tell His disciples how the GOD KIND OF FAITH works.

You and I need to know how it works. If you have faith in your heart, it is the GOD KIND OF FAITH. The Bible says in Romans 12:3, **"...God hath dealt to every man the measure of faith."** And it is the GOD KIND OF FAITH. He didn't say *"a measure"*; He said *"the measure."* It is the same measure everybody got when they were born again. *The problem is, some haven't developed it.*

THE WORD tells you how to develop your faith. **"Faith cometh by hearing, and hearing by the word of God"** (Rom. 10:17). The literal Greek says, "Faith cometh by report, and that report comes from God." Hearing what God said will build faith inside you, because He's able to perform His every declaration.

Now, Jesus tells you how to apply the *GOD KIND OF FAITH* and get it to work.

Perhaps you've tried it in all kinds of ways. You've tried it by bombarding the gates of heaven, by just praying it over and over and over, and you found that didn't work.

Well, let's see something that does work, and let's act on it. Here is what Jesus said: "For verily I say unto you, That whosoever shall say unto this mountain, Be thou removed, and be thou cast into the sea; and shall not doubt in his heart, but shall believe that those things which he saith shall come to pass; he shall have whatsoever he saith" (Mark 11:23).

He didn't say just the things you say to the mountain. He said "THOSE THINGS WHICH HE SAITH"; everything you say. You must watch what you say. You have to believe that those things that you say — everything you say —will come to pass.

That will activate the GOD KIND OF FAITH within you, and THOSE THINGS WHICH YOU SAY WILL COME TO PASS. He said, HE SHALL HAVE. He didn't say he had it then, did He?

HE SAID, *"HE SHALL HAVE WHATSOEVER HE SAITH."* One of the translations says, **"He shall have whatsoever he is saying."** In other words, it shows he's continually saying that.

The Bible says, "Let us hold fast to the profession (confession) of our faith..." (Heb. 10:23).

It didn't say, "Hold fast to your prayer." When you hold fast to the prayer, you're holding fast to your problem, because most of the time you've prayed the problem.

Turn loose of the problem and get hold of your confession. Quit praying the problem. And start saying the answer. **"For verily I say unto you, whosoever shall say unto this mountain be thou removed...."**

When you prayed and said, "Lord, the mountain's getting bigger; it's not getting any better. I've prayed, and it's not working out," you were holding on to the problem. You haven't got to the answer. You're not there yet; you are still too involved with the problem.

The answer is in the confession. The answer is in believing and confessing what the WORD SAYS. THE WORD SAYS THAT IT WILL BE REMOVED AND CAST INTO THE SEA.

We should continually affirm and confess this; "I thank God, though it looks like the mountain's getting bigger, in THE NAME OF JESUS, I see it removed by the eye of faith. *BY THE EYE OF FAITH, I SEE IT REMOVED.*"

There is creative power within you. Learn to use it wisely.

CHAPTER 3

CHRISTIAN SENSE

When you continually affirm and confess: "I thank God, though it looks like the mountain's (problem) getting bigger, it's not. In the Name of Jesus I see it removed by the eye of faith," somebody will say, "Only a nut will say that. If the mountain's still there, if the trouble is still there, and you know it's there, you can't deny its existence."

You see, sometimes when I start teaching on this some will say it sounds like *Christian Science*. One lady punched her husband in a service in Texas and said (my wife overheard them), *"That sounds like Christian Science."*

It's not Christian Science. I like what Brother Kenneth Hagin says, "IT'S CHRISTIAN SENSE"!

I don't deny the existence of the mountain. I deny the right of it to exist in my way. I don't see it as being in my way. I see it in the way THE WORD SAID IT. REMOVED.

The *WORD* says, **"The just shall live by faith"** (Heb. 10:38), and not by sight, **"We walk by faith and not by sight"** (2 Cor. 5:7). But *a lot of Christians are walking by sight, and not by faith.*

Let me give you an illustration. Suppose you are driving down a highway at 60 miles per hour. Someone pulls out three blocks ahead of you and they are right in the middle of the road, crossways. You slam on your brakes and say, "There's a car right in the middle of the road!" A car from behind hits you and suddenly there's a 10-car pile-up.

Somebody says, "What's wrong with you?"

You say, "Why there was a car in the road."

Well sure it was, but it was doing 30 m.p.h.; just two more seconds and it would have been gone.

You were going totally by what you saw. You observed what was there. Then you slammed on the brakes.

That is what a lot of Christian people are doing. "Whoo! it's still there — it's still there!" You have established it. But if you will confess its removal, *Praise God, when you get there, it's going to be gone!*

You see, if you drive your car the way you've been driving your spiritual life, you would have wrecked that thing a dozen times. You can see that.

You don't pay any attention to the car out there three blocks up the road; the computer in your head is telling you, "He's going 30 m.p.h. In two more seconds he'll be on the other side of the road. There's no danger, I'll just keep going." And you sit there, and you see that car, you never flinch, you never reach for the brakes, you just drive along perfectly at ease.

Why?

Because you have faith in what that guy's doing. You are actually believing something you are not seeing. You ARE believing the END results. Driving your car successfully is based on split second timing.

Now he may decide to just throw on his brakes right there and stop. Then you would want to know what was wrong with him!

Apply that when the *storms of life* come against you and the devil says, "Look here, you will never be able to get over that." *Just ignore him and say, "Thank God, I BELIEVE THE WORD. It will not be there when I get there."*

That kind of faith will move mountains. You may get to the foot of the mountain, sometime before it moves. It will either move, or there will be a hole come in it!

But, if you go to *"mealy-mouthing"* around and say, "I believe it's getting slower, I don't believe it's going to leave," you're in trouble.

Jesus said, "Say to the mountain *be removed* and cast into the sea."

Say what you want done with it.

Don't go to God and pray, "Dear God, it's getting worse."

HE SAID THAT YOU CAN *HAVE WHAT YOU SAY,* **and** you said, it's getting worse. *That ought to tell you something.*

Jesus said, the GOD KIND OF FAITH WORKS by the words of your mouth. There is no release of the GOD KIND OF FAITH without the WORDS OF THE MOUTH. It is *released* by the *words of your mouth.*

In Luke 17:5-6 the disciples came to Jesus and said, "Lord, increase our faith" (give us more faith). "And the Lord said, if ye had faith as a grain of mustard seed, ye might say unto this sycamine tree, Be thou plucked up by the root, and be thou planted in the sea and it should obey you." They were standing there by that tree! It probably wasn't close to a mountain. *He said that tree should obey you.* He didn't say a word about increasing their faith. In other words, He said, you've got to learn to use what you have. He said the way you use it is to start saying some things in faith.

PLANT THE SEED

Many people have desired healing. They want a harvest of healing and a harvest of physical needs met. *But they have never planted a seed.*

The law of Genesis says everything produces after its kind.

I could be the best rice farmer in the state of Arkansas, and I could sit in my house and say "Praise God, I believe in rice. My grandfather believed in rice. My daddy believed in rice. My brother believes in rice. Everybody ought to have a field of rice." I could have 10 tons of seed on my truck, waiting to be planted, but if I just sit there and praise God because I believe in rice, I'll never harvest any rice.

A lot of Christians are doing that. They're saying, "I believe the Lord's able. Yes Brother, I believe He's able to heal me."

Well, the devil knows that the Lord is able. That's no profound statement.

The thing you must determine is, WILL HE? The WORD SAYS HE WILL. Then you must start agreeing with that.

The WORD is what works. It's not our prayer that works; it's the WORD AND FAITH that works. Prayer won't make faith work.

We've thought if we just pray long enough, it would soon work out. NO, it won't. We need to get this straightened out. Faith will make prayer work, but prayer won't make faith work. FAITH WILL WORK WITHOUT PRAYER. PRAYER WON'T WORK WITHOUT FAITH.

Now, we have determined from the Word of God that you *CAN HAVE WHAT YOU SAY.* Not many people do because they have never controlled their words. Jesus said it — I didn't say it — I'm just telling you what He said. Now I'm smart enough to believe that Jesus knew what He was talking about. Jesus has made a profound statement *that you CAN HAVE WHAT YOU SAY.*

THROUGH THE KNOWLEDGE OF GOD

Let's read 2 Peter, chapter 1, starting with verse 2, "Grace and peace be multiplied unto you through the knowledge of God, and of Jesus, our Lord."

How is grace and peace going to be *multiplied* to you?

Through the *knowledge of God* and Jesus our Lord.

What is some of the knowledge of God?

How His faith works.

How does *God's* faith work?

If you find how His faith works you will know how your faith is going to work. God never did anything without saying it first, and you hardly do either. You say, "I'm going up town. I'm going to work. I'm going to do this, and I'm going to do that." You always say it before you do it. You are programmed to operate that way. So if you don't say some things in faith concerning some of the things you believe, you'll never operate in faith in those areas. The Word says in 2 Corinthians 4:13, **"We having the same spirit of faith, according as it is written, I believed, and therefore have I spoken; we also believe, and therefore speak."**

Second Peter 1:3 says, "According as his divine power hath given unto us ALL THINGS that pertain unto *life* and *godliness, through the knowledge of him* that hath called us to glory and virtue." His divine power has given unto us all things — ALL THINGS — how? through the KNOWLEDGE OF GOD.

He is saying that if you get the knowledge of God, then you have the understanding of God, the wisdom of God; and the wisdom of God is the WORD OF GOD.

Then He said that He has given to you by His divine ability all things that pertain to life and godliness. Now, if healing doesn't pertain to life, what does?

Finances also pertain to life.

Paul said, "But my God shall supply all your need according to his riches in glory by Christ Jesus" (Phil. 4:19).

Having abundant supplies to life and godliness, you ought to have abundance, in the NAME OF JESUS. The WORD says you can, if you act on the WORD OF FAITH — if you begin to do it.

Now, it won't happen overnight. That's the thing I want to bear hard on in this book. IT WON'T HAPPEN OVERNIGHT. It won't happen just because you say it one or two times.

It is going to happen because you CONTINUALLY AFFIRM WHAT GOD'S WORD SAYS — UNTIL IT

GETS INTO YOUR SPIRIT and becomes a PART OF YOU.

James 1:21 says, **"...receive with meekness the engrafted word, which is able to save your souls."** *He said the Word of God, engrafted into your spirit, will save your soul. The Word of God,* engrafted in your spirit, will deliver you from every circumstance of life.

If you have the Word for it, get it into your spirit. It will deliver you! If you will continually believe and affirm that. I don't care HOW BIG THE MOUNTAIN LOOKS! *You should not be moved by what you see. You should only be motivated by what you believe. The Word is the final authority.*

PARTAKERS OF THE DIVINE NATURE OF GOD

Second Peter 1:4 says, "Whereby (or by this, by the divine ability of God) are given unto us exceeding great and precious promises: that by these ye might be partakers of the divine nature...."

What nature?

The divine nature of God. He said you are partakers of God's nature. Praise the Lord! Partakers of God's nature.

What kind of nature does God have?

Righteousness! RIGHTEOUSNESS! Not unworthy nature, God doesn't have that, *He is Righteousness.* He said you're partakers of the righteousness of God.

"For he hath made him to be sin for us who knew no sin, that we might be made the righteousness of God in him" (2 Cor. 5:21).

The very nature of God should dominate your spirit when you are born again.

Now, it didn't say it automatically dominates your body. That is where a lot of folks have it all squirrelled up. When they were born again, they thought their body got saved; they thought their head got saved. Later they wanted to do some things that were wrong after they were born again.

The devil said, "If you were saved, you wouldn't want to do that. You must not have received anything. You must not have been saved or you wouldn't have thought those bad thoughts."

Well, I have news for you. Your head didn't get saved. Your body didn't get saved. Your spirit was born again. You were created the righteousness of God through Christ Jesus, with God on the inside.

Now, He must permeate outward, and the spirit man must bring the body into subjection to the spirit. You have to mortify some deeds of your body to go to church. To hear God's Word or to read this book, this body (flesh) has to be disciplined to the Word of God. *Your body does not always want to do the things your spirit would do.* **"For the flesh lusteth against the Spirit, and the Spirit against the flesh: and these are contrary the one to the other: so that ye cannot do the things that ye would"** (Gal. 5:17).

Sometimes your body will say, "Oh, I'd rather not," and the *spirit man* on the inside of you will say, *"Get up body, you're going."*

Either your spirit or your body is going to dominate you. And when you're born again, your spirit is supposed to dominate the body. You notice the word, "supposed" to.

Sometimes your spirit doesn't dominate because you fail to act on what you know. The Word says, **"You are partakers of the divine nature of God."** If you are **"partakers of the**

divine nature of God," and God spoke and caused creation to come into being, what do you think is going to happen when you start *saying some things in faith?*

Jesus said you can have whatsoever you say, IF you DOUBT NOT and BELIEVE in your heart the things you are speaking.

In James, chapter 3, verses 1 and 2, it says, "My brethren, be not many masters, knowing that we shall receive the greater condemnation. For in many things we offend all. If any man offend not in word, the same is a perfect man, and able also to bridle the whole body."

Now, let's read verse 2 in the Amplified version of the Bible, "For we all often stumble and fall and offend in many things. And if anyone does not offend in speech — never says the wrong things — he is a fully developed character and a perfect man, able to control his whole body and to *curb his entire nature."* Verse 3 says, "If we set bits in the horses' mouths to make them obey us, we can turn their whole bodies about."

The Greek word that has been translated "offend" in the King James version of the Bible is translated "stumble" in the Amplified version. **"For in many things we** stumble." — "**If any man stumble not in word....**" Now doesn't that change the meaning of the situation? If you don't stumble in your wording, he said — *THE SAME IS A PERFECT MAN AND ABLE TO BRING HIS WHOLE NATURE INTO OBEDIENCE.*

You can understand that. We have stumbled with our words.

Now, verse 3 in the King James version says, "**Behold, we put bits in the horses' mouths, that they may obey us; and we turn about their whole body.**" *He said the thing that is in the horse's mouth causes that whole horse to turn in any direction. Verses 4-6 say,* "**Behold also the ships, which though they be so great, and are driven of fierce winds, yet are they turned about with a very small helm, whithersoever the governor listeth. Even so the tongue is a little member, and boasteth great things. Behold, how great a matter a little fire kindleth! And the tongue is a fire, a world of iniquity: so is the *tongue among our members, that it defileth the whole body, and setteth on fire the course of nature; and it is set on fire of hell.***"

The same verse in the Amplified version says, "If we set bits in horses' mouths to make them obey us, we can turn their whole bodies about. Likewise look at the ships, though they are so great and are driven by rough winds, they are steered by a very small rudder wherever the impulse of the helmsman determines. Even so the tongue is a little member, and it can boast of great things. See how much wood or how great a forest a tiny spark can set ablaze! And the tongue is a fire. The *tongue* is a world of wickedness set among our members, contaminating and depriving the whole body and setting on fire the wheel of birth — the cycle of man's nature — being itself ignited by hell (Gehenna)."

Let me tell you in common words what he's saying. He said you could put bits in a horse's mouth and turn his whole body. He said a great big ship weighing hundreds of thousands of tons is turned to any direction by just a very small rudder on the back of it, wherever the captain decides to turn it. He goes on and says the tongue is a fire, a world of iniquity. So is the tongue, so put among our members that it can defile the whole body, and it setteth on fire the course of nature, or as the Amplified says,

"…the wheel of our birth, cycle of man's nature…." That means if you have inherited good health from your parents, if your grandfather was healthy, if good health just generally runs in your family, then more than likely you will be healthy. When you buy an insurance policy you must have a medical examination. The doctor will ask you how healthy your parents and grandparents were, and did they die with this or that. They can tell a lot about how long you're going to live from the answers to those questions.

Now, the Word says that the *tongue* can stop those natural forces. The *tongue* can destroy the very course of nature that causes you to be healthy.

If you begin to say, "I believe I'm coming down with something," you probably will.

"I believe I am taking a cold."

You'll get it!

I've had people come in the prayer line and say, "I'm afraid I've got cancer. Well, I don't have any proof, but I just believe I've got it."

It says the *tongue will set on fire the course of nature.* It will destroy the life-giving flow in you that God put in you to heal you and make you whole.

Everyone has natural healing power within their body. If you cut your finger, you don't have to be concerned about it. It knows how to heal itself. *That healing power is in you.*

If you go to talking sickness and disease and defeat, you have released words that will produce after their kind. You can stop the natural healing power that God put in you by the words of your mouth. Many have stopped divine healing the same way, by negative words.

Verses 7-8 say, "...every kind of beasts, and of birds, and serpents, and of things in the sea is tamed, and hath been tamed of mankind: But the tongue can no man tame...."

Someone said, "See there is no use trying. The Bible says you can't tame it, *no man can tame the tongue.*

The Amplified says, "But the human tongue can be tamed by no man and it is an undisciplined, and irreconcilable restless evil, full of death-bringing poison."

And you know, you've got that thing in your mouth!

He said, the tongue no man can tame. It is an unruly evil that's full of deadly poison. It will poison your body. It will poison your spirit. It will poison your life. OR, it will put you over in life, if used correctly. It will build life and health into spirit, soul, and body.

He *said* no man could tame it, but thank God, *THE HOLY SPIRIT CAN!*

Some have said, "What's so good in all that talking in tongues anyway?"

Then, many believe it went out with the apostles.

Well, did you see the life of Peter? He was always spouting off at the mouth and saying what he would do. "...I'd die for you," he said.

Well I guess so, Jesus was standing right there.

"Yeah, I'll die for you."

Later someone said, "I believe that man's one of them," and tried to accuse Peter of being a follower of Jesus, accused him of being a Christian. But they couldn't find enough evidence to convict him.

"No," Peter said, "I don't know the man." Those words came right out of his mouth. *He didn't have control of his tongue. It was dominated by fear.*

AFTER THE DAY OF PENTECOST

But after the day of Pentecost when Peter was baptized in the Holy Ghost and spoke with tongues, the power of God came inside him. Then Peter stood up and talked three minutes and three thousand souls were saved! There was POWER IN HIS WORDS! Then he walked out of the upper room and the first crippled man he came to, he said (paraphrased), "I don't have any money, my wife keeps the money, but what I've got, I'm going to give you, IN THE NAME OF JESUS RISE UP AND WALK" (Acts 3:6).

That old boy's eyes got big and he said, "Nobody's ever talked to me like that. Everybody always said, "Oh bless your heart; it'll be worth it all some day. You're just 'suffering for the Lord.' God's trying to teach you something."

And when Peter said, "such as I have, I give you, and in the Name of Jesus, get up and walk," he said, "I don't know what it is, but I WANT IT, PRAISE GOD!"

Peter took him by the hand and up he came!

Peter learned to control his tongue. I don't ever see where Peter got in any more trouble by his rash talking after the day of Pentecost. *That ought to tell us something.* The power of God started operating in Peter's life after he was baptized with the Holy Ghost. *The Holy Ghost tamed his tongue.*

He will tame yours if you will let Him; if you will take heed to the Word of God. *The Holy Spirit works on man from the inside out.*

Then from what James said you see, WHAT YOU SAY CAN CAUSE SICKNESS AND DISEASE, or IT CAN STOP IT. You can drive sickness and disease out of your body with the WORDS OF YOUR MOUTH.

Someone said, "Now that sounds like POSITIVE THINKING or CHRISTIAN SCIENCE."

No, it's not Christian Science. I don't deny the existence of disease. I deny the right of that disease to exist in this body, because I'm the Body of Christ. **"Now ye are the body of Christ, and members in particular"** (1 Cor. 12:27).

SICKNESS A CURSE

The Word says, "Christ hath redeemed us from the curse of the law, being made a curse for us: for it is written, Cursed is every one that hangeth on a tree: That the blessing of Abraham might come on the Gentiles through Jesus Christ; that we might receive the promise of the Spirit through faith" (Gal. 3:13,14).

All sickness and disease is under the curse, "Also every sickness, and every plague, which is not written in the book of this law, them will the Lord bring upon thee, until thou be destroyed" (Deut. 28:61). But, praise God! *Christ redeemed us from the curse of the law.*

I can't see where Jesus was ever sick until He became a curse for us on the cross. He was the body of Christ while He was here on earth, but now you are a member of the Body of Christ. Therefore, when sickness or disease tries to fasten itself upon your body, you should make this confession: "I'm the *Body of Christ*, I am *redeemed from the curse*, and I forbid any sickness or disease to operate in this body. Every organ, every tissue of this body functions in the perfection to which God created it to function. Every organ, every tissue will function properly, *for greater is He that is in me than he that is in the world*."

CHAPTER 4

ESTABLISHING THE WORD OF GOD

I have heard some folks say, "Pray for me, I'm taking the *flu.*"

They've got it *termed right*; they are *taking it.* Satan offered it to them. He said, "You've got a runny nose, and a neck ache; now, let's see what you're going to say about it." Then most people will side with the devil and begin to say the very thing he said. "I am taking a cold."

The WORD says, "...In the mouth of two or three witnesses shall every word be established" (2 Cor. 13:1).

You may have a runny nose. You may have aches all over. That is how you feel, but what are you going to say about it?

God's Word is forever settled in heaven; it is already established there. **"For ever, O Lord, thy word is settled in heaven"** (Ps. 119:89).

The first thing most people do is to go tell their wife or husband, "I believe I'm taking the flu." *You have released faith in sickness. You have established the words of the enemy. And Jesus said you can have what you say.* The WORD, in essence, said the *tongue will cause the healing power to stop.* It will set on fire the wheels of lineage, or that which you have inherited. What you have *inherited is natural healing power in your body.* Now don't misunderstand me. I am not talking about *divine healing* at this point, but the *natural healing ability of the human body.* Then all things being level, all things being right, and without Satan involved, any sickness that comes upon your body —your body will cast it off and heal itself.

That healing ability is in your body. But Satan has come on the scene, and he distorts these things, and *he has found out that his ability is limited to what he can get you to say.*

Jesus said you can have what you say. Not many Christians know that, but Satan knows that, and he believes it.

Just think back to the last time you had a cold or were sick. What was the first thing you wanted to do after you noticed the symptoms?

You wanted to go tell somebody, "I'm sick." And you probably did. Then you began to get worse immediately if not sooner. Being unaware, you activated a spiritual law that gave the authority you had to dominate your physical body over to the enemy. You established the words of the enemy instead of God's Word. You have openly proclaimed, I AM SICK.

HEALING POWER OF THE WORD

I beg your pardon, *THE WORD SAYS YOU'RE HEALED.* "Who his own self bare our sins in his own body on the tree, that we, being dead to sins, should live unto righteousness: by whose stripes ye were healed" (1 Peter 2:24). *Not going to be — WERE HEALED —* Jesus already did it two thousand years ago. He's not going to do any more to heal you.

You lay hold on what He said and deny that sickness has the right to exist in your body. Lay hold upon it by faith, confess the WORD OF GOD over it, and say, "I may hurt, but in the NAME OF JESUS I AM HEALED."

Somebody said, "That sounds like a *nut*!"

Well, it may, but I'd rather be a well nut than a *sick one!* It works. It works because God said it would. God tells you in His Word YOU CAN HAVE WHAT YOU SAY.

Most people are having what they say, but they say the wrong things. Now, a lady stood up in the church and said, *"Pray for me, I'm taking the flu."* Your praying wouldn't do her any good. *You're wasting your time praying for her. She believes the wrong thing. By the words of her mouth she has released faith in the ability of the enemy to make her sick. She has no Scripture basis for that belief. She has been motivated by her physical feelings.*

The just shall live by faith and not by sight.

We should learn to believe more in what God's Word says rather than our feelings. Feelings change from day to day.

The Word of God never changes. It always stays the same, regardless of how you feel.

How you feel has nothing to do with God performing His Word.

I've seen people ask the pastor to "Come over and pray for me." The pastor would go over and I would go with him, and we would pray for them, and say, "Do you believe you are healed?"

And they would say, "Well, I hope so."

Well, they aren't. No need fooling yourself. There was no faith in that. Hoping won't get it. *Hope has no substance.*

The Bible said, "...The prayer of faith shall save the sick, and the Lord shall raise him up..." (James 5:15).

Somebody said, "Yeah, but I still hurt after they *got through praying.*"

Their faith was based totally on feelings, not on the WORD. It didn't say the prayer of faith will heal the sick if they don't hurt after prayer. It says, **"The prayer of faith shall save the sick; and the Lord WILL raise him up."**

We should say, "Thank God they prayed. I believe they prayed in faith and I know I believed God. Therefore, I'm getting up IN THE NAME OF JESUS."

We have pampered these things.

Now I'm not fighting doctors, don't misunderstand me. If you haven't learned to operate in this, go on to your doctor. He is your very best friend. *Doctors are fighting the same evil with medical means. There is nothing wrong with going to your doctor. But learn to operate in the ABILITY OF GOD. Release the ability of God in you by the FAITH-FILLED WORDS of your mouth.*

James said YOU CAN do it. He said if you can control the tongue you would have no trouble with the body. He said the tongue is to the physical body (THE RULING FACTOR) as bits are to a horse. They are both in the mouth, and they also have control of the physical body. He said, if you would control the tongue, you would not have any trouble with the body.

THE BODY WILL OBEY WORDS.

THE BODY HAS TO BE TRAINED TO ACT UPON THE WORD OF GOD.

YOUR BODY OBEYS THE COMMAND OF YOUR MIND.

You start saying this, "I don't desire to eat so much that I become overweight, because this body is the temple of the Holy Ghost; therefore, in the Name of Jesus, I do not desire to eat more than this body needs. And in the Name of Jesus, I refuse to overeat."

Start confessing that into your diet program. When you start using words to *triumph* instead of allowing them to *hold you in bondage, they will work for you. Your words will work for you.*

Now, it won't work because you said it once. I didn't say that. I said start confessing it. Start confessing the things you desire, not the problems that exist.

Somebody said, "How long do I have to confess it?"

Until you get the desired results. You see, He said control the words of your mouth.

You have been confessing this, "Oh, I know I've had enough, but I sure DO WANT a piece of pie. I just love pie. I can't do without sweets. I guess I will get as big as a barn."

I have actually heard people say that. You said it with your mouth, "I want a piece of pie." Your body starts desiring it right then. *You build desires with words. Your body may have been trained in this manner. Mortify those desires by saying, "No, in the Name of Jesus, I don't desire any more food than I need."*

Somebody said, "Well, that would be lying."

No, that's the spirit man talking. He is programmed with the WORD OF GOD, and the spirit man says, "I don't desire anything that would be harmful to the body. I know that if I overeat, it will be harmful to the body; therefore, I'm speaking out of the spirit man and saying, 'I don't desire anymore in the Name of Jesus!'"

Now you have set a law in motion. You have done something to your body. You've said to your body, "Now, just settle down and you conform to the WORD OF GOD, IN THE NAME OF JESUS."

Yes, talk to it. Now I would advise you to do it quietly when in public, because people will give you a lot of room if they hear you!

Jesus always spoke TO the problem. He spoke the desired results, the end results. We would be wise to follow His example.

I want you to see what Jesus had to say concerning this subject. "Either make the tree good, and his fruit good; or else make the tree corrupt, and his fruit corrupt: for the tree is known by his fruit. O generation of vipers, how can ye, being evil, speak good things? for out of the abundance of the heart the mouth speaketh" (Matt. 12:33,34).

Now, Jesus told us a profound truth. You speak out of your mouth what is abundant in your heart.

The symptoms came and the devil said, "I wonder what you've got?"

You said, "I don't know. I wonder what I've got?"

He got out his little *flip chart* and said, "Do you believe you've got the *flu?*"

"Now, I don't believe I have the flu."

"Well, do you believe you have a bad sore throat?"

"Well, yeah, my throat does feel kind of raw." YOU MUST MAKE A DECISION. Will you be motivated by what you feel, see, or hear, or the WORD? The Word said Jesus bore your sickness. (Matt. 8:17.)

Isaiah 53:5 says, "...With his stripes we ARE healed."

You begin to rationalize, "I sure don't feel healed. I really don't look like I'm healed because my throat looks red. I really don't sound healed; my voice is getting raspy."

The physical has won out over the WORD OF GOD. "Honey, I'm sick." Your voice penetrates every fiber of your being, even to your heart (spirit). Your tongue, the high authority, the controlling factor of the body and spirit, has declared it to be so and all resistance to that virus ceases. YOU ARE INDEED SICK.

You may say, "Yeah, but I was feeling bad before I ever said that."

Yes, the symptoms came. *But the enemy can't put anything on you without your consent.* Now he can cause you to feel like it's coming on. See, you go back to feeling there. That's why it's dangerous to live by your five physical senses — what you feel, see, hear, taste, and touch.

PROGRAM YOURSELF
BY THE WORD

Learn to program yourself by the Word. When you feel bad, say, "Now what does the Word say about that? Well, praise the Lord, the Word says, '**By his stripes, I'm healed.**' Therefore I won't receive your sickness, Satan. I just *pass it up*, thank you."

If someone came to your door and offered you a sack of rattlesnakes, would you just back off and say, "Well I guess it's the will of the Lord. Just dump them right here in the living room. Oh dear God, what am I going to do with these snakes? Snakes in the pantry, snakes in the bathroom, snakes everywhere. Well, I guess this is *my cross to bear.*"

Well, dummy, you could have stopped it at the door! *Be smart enough to shut the door! Say,* "No, thank you, I don't want any."

Don't get up and testify to the whole church, "I'm taking the flu."

One night, I heard a lady just announce it to the whole church, *"I'm taking the flu,"* and most of the people in the congregation said, "You know, she does look bad. You know, I did notice her eyes watering. *Yeah, she's taking the flu. That's what it is.*"

Now she has a hundred people agreeing she has the flu.

And Jesus said, "If two of you shall agree on earth... (Matt. 18:19).

Wouldn't it be much simpler to stand up and say, "Well, the enemy's been trying to put the symptoms of the *flu* on me and cause me to *believe* in it. But I stand before you tonight, and you are my witnesses before the angels and before God and before heaven *that I AM not sick. I'll not have the flu — by the stripes of Jesus, I'm healed.* That settles it, thank you. *The Word says I'm healed. That's good enough for me."*

There would be folks with *goggle eyes,* saying, "I wonder what's wrong with her?"

But when the woman stood up and said, "I'm taking the flu," nobody snickered. They just said, "Oh, poor thing! Yes, she's taking the *flu."*

Can you see how *dumb* we've been when it comes to these things?

Now I didn't always see this. Don't think I'm saying, "I know all the answers." I don't have them all yet, but thank God, I'm getting them from the WORD OF GOD!

Remember, Jesus said, **"...Out of the abundance of the heart the mouth speaketh"** (Matt. 12:34). That *sickness* and *disease* got in your *spirit* before it came out of your mouth. *It was received into your spirit first. Then as you believed you spoke.* **"We having the same spirit of faith, according as it is written, I believed, and therefore have I spoken; we also believe, and therefore speak"** (2 Cor. 4:13).

James said, **It'll set on fire the course of nature.** It will stop the ABILITY OF GOD (Divine Healing) from being released within you. It will put you in bondage unless you learn to control the words of your mouth. **"Thou art snared with the words of thy mouth, thou art taken with the words of thy mouth"** (Prov. 6:2).

A MESSAGE OF DELIVERANCE

God gave you a message of deliverance. He said, *"You can have what you say* if you *believe* in your *heart* and *doubt not."* And He said, "Out of the abundance of the heart the mouth speaketh." That ought to tell us something.

In Matthew, chapter 15, and starting with verse 11, they were complaining to Jesus about His disciples eating without washing their hands. Wasn't that a big deal? He said, **"Not that which goeth into the mouth defileth a man; but that which cometh out of the mouth, this defileth a man."** Let's look at verse 18. **"But those things which proceed out of the mouth come forth *from the heart*; and *they defile the man.*"** Jesus is saying, what you speak out of your mouth is in your heart, and when it comes out, it is set in motion. *It has established your witness on the earth.* The Word says, **"...in the mouth of two or three witnesses shall every word be established"** (2 Cor. 13:1).

The Word says you are healed.

The devil says you're sick.

You got up and said, "I'm sick."

YOU JUST ESTABLISHED IT BY THE WORDS OF YOUR MOUTH. YOU AGREED WITH THE ENEMY.

You could have just as well said, "No, just pass me up, thank you, I won't receive it."

He said the words of your mouth will defile you.

James said the tongue can defile the whole body.

CREATE A DIFFERENT WORLD THAT YOU LIVE IN

Creative power was in God's mouth. It is in your mouth also. Now that doesn't mean you're going to go out and create a world. But you can create a different world that you live in by the words of your mouth, by speaking FAITH-FILLED WORDS instead of speaking words of fear.

Fear is the reverse gear of faith.

Fear is produced by believing wrong things.

Fear is faith in the enemy's ability.

Jesus said, "A good man out of the good treasure of the heart bringeth forth good things..." (Matt. 12:35).

Where do the *good things* of life come from?

Jesus said they come out of your heart. He didn't say they come from staying up late hours and working your fingers to the bones. He said the *good things* of life *come out of your heart,* whatever you store there, the *information you program your spirit with will produce for you. It always produces after its kind. Faith produces faith. Fearful words produce fear in abundance.*

When I talk about the *spirit,* I'm talking about the *heart.* The heart and the spirit are the same. The way you program your spirit with the *WORD OF GOD* is by saying the thing God said about you in His Word. *Imitate God. Say the SAME THING* He said. Resist the devil and he will flee from you.

One of the chronic problems in the church world today is failing to recognize the *authority of the WORD.* At the first symptom of sickness you hear them say, "I am sick."

James 4:7 says, **"Submit yourselves therefore to God. Resist the devil, and he will flee from you."** To be submitted to God is to be submitted to His Word. YOU be submitted to God. YOU be submitted to His Word.

Jesus resisted Satan with the *spoken word.* Matthew chapter 4, verses 4, 7 and 10 say, "But he answered and said, It is written, Man shall not live by bread alone, but by every word that proceedeth out of the mouth of God." Verse 7, "Jesus said unto him, It is written again, Thou shalt not tempt the Lord thy God." Verse 10, "Then saith Jesus unto him; Get thee hence, satan: for it is written, Thou shalt worship the Lord thy God, and him only shalt thou serve." He spoke to Satan and he left.

HE BARE OUR SICKNESS AND SIN

Let's read 1 Peter 2:24, "Who his own self bare our sins in his own body on the tree, that we, being dead to sins, should live unto righteousness: by whose stripes ye were healed."

The WORD says you were healed. Sickness is a curse of the law, and Galatians 3:13 says, "Christ hath redeemed us from the curse of the law, being made a curse for us...." Matthew 8:17 says, "That it might be fulfilled which was spoken by Esaias the prophet, saying, Himself took our infirmities, and bare our sicknesses." He took *your* infirmities and bare your sicknesses. Learn to read the scriptures with a personal identification. Isaiah 53:5 says, "...with his stripes we are healed." *With His stripes YOU ARE HEALED.*

Someone said, "Yes, but you don't understand. I don't feel healed and I really don't look healed."

That person has been programmed by the world system, the five physical senses. *The WORD is not IN them.* They may know about the WORD, they may even believe the Word is true, but until it becomes a part of them, it is not in them.

Yes, I do understand. You are motivated by your feelings and not by the WORD of GOD.

It is very simple to resist the devil, once you have been programmed by the WORD of GOD. *God and His WORD are one. They agree.*

Learn to rise to the level of God's Word by quoting what God said. Then you can boldly say, "According to the Word of God, I am not sick. Jesus took my sickness, He bore it for me; therefore *I receive my healing through the Word.*"

Just as sure as Jesus bore your sins, He also bore your sickness. You have no more right to allow sickness to operate in your body than you do sin.

DEVELOP YOUR FAITH

If you have not developed your faith in the Word to the level where you can receive your healing through the Word, then *use medical science's healing,* but don't allow sickness and disease to lord it over you. Use whatever means you must to get rid of it, but don't let it dominate you. If you have to take pills to get your healing, then every time you have to take one, say, "I take this pill in the Name of Jesus." You will find the Name of Jesus will make your pills work twice as good.

Don't let Satan condemn you over taking medicine. God wants you well. If your faith is not developed to that point, for God's sake, don't suffer 39 years and say you trusted the Lord. No—if you suffered 39 years you missed it somewhere. That is not God's will for you. Get some medical help, get back on your feet, then get in the WORD of God and find out where you missed it. Learn to control circumstances, instead of allowing them to control you.

A few years ago a man said to me, "I wouldn't ask you to pray for me; I am taking medicine."

You can see how Satan has conned many good Christians into believing that if they are taking medicine they wouldn't *dare use prayer too.* He realizes he can't keep you from using both so he set out to convince you that *prayer* and *medicine* are opposed to each other. The *truth* is both *prayer and medicine are fighting the same evil* (sickness and diseases).

Of course, *God's best for you is for you to develop your faith* to the point that you receive healing through prayer and the Word of God. But not everyone's faith is developed to that level. That is one of the reasons God gave men medical knowledge. *He wants people well even though they don't know how to operate in the Word.*

GOD WANTS YOU WELL

Say this right now, "GOD WANTS ME WELL" (3 John 2).

Say it again, loud, "GOD WANTS ME WELL."

Confess God's Word to your body daily. Yes — talk to it. Sometimes your body wants to be sick. Don't let it. Jesus said you can have what you say, so take time to fill your heart (spirit) with God's Word.

GOD'S WORD PRODUCES FAITH

I have had people come in the prayer line and say, "Pray for me that I will have more faith." The real problem is a lack of the Word in their heart. You see, faith cometh by hearing the Word of God. It is unscriptural to pray that you will have more faith. *God's Word is filled with faith.* Where His Word is — Faith is. **"If ye abide in me, and my words abide in you, ye shall ask what ye will, and it shall be done unto you"** (John 15:7).

When the Word is absent, faith is absent.

When you come under the pressure of life, that which is abundantly in your heart is going to come out, whether it is God's Word or Satan's.

Satan's words produce fear and unbelief in your heart.

God's Word produces faith in your heart.

And "...out of the abundance of the heart the mouth speaketh" (Matt. 12:34).

That which is formed by the tongue and spoken out of the mouth, those words, will either create good or evil. They have creative power. **"A good man out of the good treasure of the heart bringeth forth good things: and an evil man out of the evil treasure bringeth forth evil things"** (Matt. 12:35). **"But those things which proceed out of the mouth come forth from the heart; and they defile the man. For out of the heart proceed evil thoughts, murders, adulteries, fornications, thefts, false witness, blasphemies: These are the things which defile a man..."** (Matt. 15:18-20).

Words conceived in your heart *will be formed by your tongue,* and by speaking them out of your mouth you will either release the ability of Satan or the ABILITY OF GOD within you. Those words will create good or evil, curse or blessing. **"Out of the same mouth proceedeth blessing and cursing..."** (James 3:10).

There is creative power within you. Learn to use it wisely.

The Spirit of God spoke to me one morning, and He said, "You don't have to worry about establishing my Word in heaven— it's already established there. What you need to do is ESTABLISH IT ON EARTH. Establish MY WORD on earth. Get it established down there, and you won't have any problem." He said, "The problem is that you have been establishing the devil's word. You've been saying what the enemy said."

ESTABLISH GOD'S WORD HERE ON EARTH.

CHAPTER 5

MY PERSONAL
FIGHT OF FAITH

Several years ago I invested quite a large sum of money in a *joint business venture.* I had *put out* a *fleece* before the Lord about this business deal. Well, all the *fleeces turned out* just the way I asked. *But I really got fleeced.* You see, Paul said in 2 Corinthians 4:4, **"In whom the god of this world hath blinded the minds of them which believe not, lest the light of the glorious gospel of Christ, who is the image of God, should shine unto them."** Paul said, Satan is the god of this *physical world,* and he knew the *fleece* I had *put out.*

Now I have found a better way to find the will of God. "Howbeit when he, the *Spirit of truth,* is come, *he will*

81

guide you into all truth: for he shall not speak of himself; but whatsoever he shall hear, that shall he speak: and he will shew you things to come" (John 16:13).

I had sold a small farm and invested the money in this business. I lost nearly all the original investment plus $25,000 more.

Through the confusion the enemy caused, *I lost faith and turned negative on life.* I thought God had done this to me. That was what Satan had put in my mind. After several months, I realized that the *negative thoughts* in my mind did not agree with the *Word of God.*

Then the enemy tried to convince me that I had failed God and that was the reason I had lost the money, and God was mad at me.

I know this story sounds familiar to many, because it is one of Satan's favorite lies that he uses to bring condemnation and confusion to God's people.

MY CONFESSIONS RULED

In that confused state of mind I turned negative. I began to say, "It doesn't matter what I do, it won't work out anyway."

I was still farming about 800 acres of land at that time, so I turned my attention to the farming operation. I knew that was one thing I could do well because I had always been successful in it.

But after I had *turned negative*, I would plant cotton and say, "Well, it doesn't make any difference how deep I plant it, it will probably rain three inches and it won't come up anyway."

It did rain and the cotton didn't come up.

I planted again, this time shallow, about one-half inch deep, and told almost everyone I saw, "Now it will turn off dry and won't rain for three weeks."

And it did just what I said.

The third time I planted that year, I made more *negative statements*. The more problems showed up the more negative I became (this is Satan's cycle). The third planting

I produced about two-thirds of a stand of cotton. I can, even now, still hear my words. "Now there will probably come an early freeze and kill it before it opens."

And it did.

For two whole years I confessed the same thing and got just what I said. I farmed that 800 acres those two years and did not make enough money to buy my driver's license. The farming practices that once worked for me did not work. The same ground that once produced bounteously now refused to respond.

I was still giving. I still believed Luke 6:38, *"Give, and it shall be given unto you; good measure, pressed down, and shaken together, and running over, shall men give into your bosom. For with the same measure that ye mete withal it shall be measured to you again."* But it was not working for me. *I prayed, I repented, I begged God to prosper me, but nothing worked. I was still negative. My confession destroyed my prayer. I saw failure everywhere I looked. I believed it and confessed it daily. I was a failure.* I was at the end of the rope so to speak, financially. I had just borrowed $100,000 to pay my back bills. I was so poor I couldn't pay attention. That's the truth. I would go to church, but I couldn't get anything out of the service because I was worrying about my finances.

Then a Baptist man came to my house one day. He had some books with him. I remember thumbing through one of the books and reading a few paragraphs here and there.

The title of the book was *Right and Wrong Thinking,* by Kenneth Hagin. It was different from any book I had ever read. Every paragraph said something, and it was straight to the point. I remember to this day one of the first statements I read. "*People that think wrong believe wrong, and when they believe wrong, they act wrong.*"

It went off inside me like a bombshell. It just seemed like someone turned a light on inside me. **"The entrance of thy words giveth light; it giveth understanding unto the simple"** (Ps. 119:130). *I knew instantly that this was truth.*

I ordered that book and another one on *"Confessions."* I began to *dig* into the Word of God to see where I was missing it. I had never heard anyone preach on Mark 11:23-24, **"For verily I say unto you, That whosoever shall say unto this mountain, Be thou removed, and be thou cast into the sea; and shall not doubt in his heart, but shall believe that those things which he saith shall come to**

pass; he shall have whatsoever he saith. Therefore I say unto you, What things soever ye desire, when ye pray, believe that ye receive them, and ye shall have them."

I am sure I had read it but it meant nothing to me. It was not in me. I had no idea you could have what you say. But as I began to *prayerfully study* what Jesus said about *WORDS*, the mouth, and prayer, God began to reveal these things to me.

I remember one morning I was praying and I said, "Father, I have prayed and *it is not working out.*"

He spoke inside my spirit just as plain, "What are you doing?"

I said, "I am praying."

He said, "No, you're not, you are complaining." Then He said, "Who told you it is not working out?"

Now that shook me. I thought for a minute, then I said, *"Well, I guess the devil said that."*

Then He spoke into my spirit some things that totally transformed my life. He said, *"I would appreciate it if you would quit telling Me what the devil said.* Now you have been praying for Me to prosper you and get the devil off of you. I am not the One who is causing your problems. You are under an attack of the evil one and I can't do anything about it. *You have bound Me by the words of your own mouth.* And it is not going to get any better until you change your confessions and begin to agree with My Word. *You are operating in fear and unbelief. You have established the words of the evil one in your behalf.* By your own mouth you have released the ability of the enemy; and if I did anything about it, I would have to violate My Word, and I can't do that."

You see, I had just gotten enough of His Word in me to where He could talk to me intelligently about the problem. *Until then He had no basis on which to talk to me for I had cast out His Word and quoted the enemy.* Over a period of the next few months He spoke many things into my spirit that totally *upended my way of thinking,* some of which I will share in a later book.

He said, "I am for you. I want you to prosper, but I want you to do it in a way that will work an eternal value in you, by using your faith and acting on the Word. The power of binding and loosing is not in heaven. It is on earth, and if you don't do it, it won't be done."

Then He told me this, "Study and search my Word for promises that pertain to you as a believer. Make a list of these and confess them aloud daily. *They will build into your spirit over a period of time. Then when these truths are established in your spirit they will become true in you.*"

SECRET OF FAITH

This is the secret of faith, continually saying what God said. So, for two and one-half years I studied the Word of God and made my confession list.

Many people want to know why it won't work for them when they have not *meditated* the *Word* and would not dare say anything contrary to their *sense knowledge.* They would not dare say, "My God has supplied all my need according to His riches by Christ Jesus," when the rent is due and they don't have the money. Sense knowledge would say that would be telling a lie.

But how can you tell a lie when you say the truth?

GOD'S WORD IS TRUTH. "But my God shall supply all your need according to his riches...by Christ Jesus" (Phil. 4:19).

The Lord spoke to me about going on a *Word fast* for two weeks. I didn't read anything but the Word of God or something pertaining to the Word. I didn't watch any television, not even a news program for two weeks. I was so excited about the Word at the end of those two weeks that I haven't really cared about reading a newspaper or watching T.V. since.

I began a process of training my spirit with the Word of God.

One day as I was confessing "the devil flees from me because I resist him in Jesus' name," I suddenly realized that the anointing of God was rising up in me. My spirit had received it and now it was being manifest in me. In an instant of time I knew the devil was fleeing from me and my words took on authority.

God's Words are filled with faith and that is how faith comes.

It didn't come by watching the *Doctors,* or *Gunsmoke,* it came by the *WORD* of God. Understand — this process of training the human spirit did not work overnight. I didn't say it one day and be full of faith the next. *It was a process of weeding out religious tradition from the WORD.*

TRAINING THE HUMAN SPIRIT

Tradition says, "If you feel sick you are not healed."

But I chose the WORD.

Tradition says, "If you pray and it looks worse keep bombarding the gates of heaven."

But the WORD says, "When you pray believe you receive them and you shall."

So, I would go to the *WORD* to see what the *WORD* said about it. Then I would pray what the *Word SAID*, **"My God supplieth all my need according to *HIS RICHES*."**

PRAYER became a challenging experience of forgetting circumstances. It was exciting to confess I have abundance and there is no lack, when the lack was very apparent.

"The Lord is my shepherd, I do not want," when want was all around.

"No weapon formed against me will prosper," when it looked like everything that came along was working against me and prospering very well.

One morning as I was confessing the WORD, I stopped and said, "Lord, You know I don't believe all this I am saying is true in me." (It was that tradition coming through that made me feel like I was lying.) *I knew the Bible was true and it was in the Bible.*

The Lord said, "That's all right, son. Just keep saying what the WORD says until it becomes a part of you, then it will be true in you."

So I kept confessing, "I have abundance and no lack; my God supplieth all my need," until it was formed in my spirit and became a part of me. *Then, I realized I had broken into a realm of faith that I never knew existed.*

A NEW REALM OF FAITH

"If ye abide in me, and my words abide in you, ye shall ask what ye will, and it shall be done unto you" (John 15:7). I could now make those statements with full assurance that God would honor His Word. It was a strange feeling on the inside of me. In my spirit I knew I had abundance, yet I could plainly see with the natural eyes it was not manifest.

I had prayed and asked the Father for some more land. I said, "I don't know where there is any land available, but I know You do, and I ask You in the Name of Jesus to cause it to come to me. I see in Your Word where You said the angels were ministering spirits sent forth to minister for them who are heirs of salvation. Therefore, I say the ministering spirits will begin to work and cause the land to come to me in Jesus' name."

I was excited about positive prayer, and I never prayed about that again. I began to praise God for the answer.

About two weeks had passed and I had really not even thought about it. *I had considered it done when I prayed.* That morning the phone rang. When I answered, the party told me who she was and said, "We are going to sell our farm. Do you want to buy it?"

It caught me by surprise because I knew many people had tried to buy small plots from them to no avail. I know I stuttered but finally said, "Yes, I would."

I made an appointment to meet with them that night.

As I hung up the phone my wife said, *"What are you going to do?"*

I said, "I am going to buy the farm."

She kind of laughed and said, "What are you going to use for money?"

The next sentence came right out of my spirit. "Money is no problem." I just stood there goggle-eyed at what I had said. It had to come out of my spirit because my head knew I didn't have any money. But my spirit was programmed to abundance.

My oldest daughter was standing there, and we all three *joined hands, agreed,* and *said* with our mouths, *"The farm is ours in the Name of Jesus."*

The day that followed proved to be very trying to that *faith statement,* but we would not negate that statement. Oh, I wanted to, sometimes very badly, but I would shut my mouth and not say it.

This is where the fight of faith is lost so many times, just one inch below the nose (the mouth).

In one of those trying hours I was driving home, and from all outward circumstances it looked as though the farm was going to another person. I was praying in the spirit (in tongues) and the Spirit of God spoke up on the inside of me and said, *"Go speak to the mountain."*

I knew who the mountain was, another man bidding for the farm. I didn't know what to say but I confessed, *"The Spirit of truth abideth in me and teaches me all things and I have the mind of Christ."*

I talked to the man and he said, "I don't really need the farm. If you want it I will withdraw my bid."

He withdrew his bid and the *mountain* was removed! They sold me the farm.

(MARK 4:15) — SATAN CAME TO STEAL THE WORD

I had made arrangements for the finances, but when I started to close the deal the lending agency said they had made a mistake and could not loan the money.

This was the enemy's way of saying, "Will you accept defeat?"

Again — it looked as if all was lost. I didn't have any money to pay down on the farm. I was operating on borrowed money. As I sat there, hearing the words that a few years before would have caused me to say, "Well, I knew it was too good to be true, nothing ever works out for me," the Holy Spirit spoke up on the inside and said, *"Go across the street to the bank."*

Now that sounded silly to my head, because I had never done any banking at that bank. It was not in my hometown. However, I did know the president of the bank.

So I walked across to the bank. As I walked in the door the president of the bank said, "Hi, what can we do for you?"

I was direct to the point, "I need to borrow 'X' number of dollars." It was a figure greater than I had ever borrowed at one time.

He said, "Well, bring the papers. I heard about that farm you bought. We will loan you the whole amount if you want it."

It seemed as though I could hear my words still hanging in the air, *"MONEY IS NO PROBLEM. I will buy the farm,"* spoken nearly a month before. But they had become creative power formed out of the image of the Word of God.

THE TONGUE: A CREATIVE FORCE

"...and whatsoever he doeth shall prosper" (Ps.1:3).

"No weapon that is formed against thee shall prosper" (Isa. 54:17).

"But my God shall supply all your need according to his riches in glory by Christ Jesus" (Phil. 4:19).

"The Lord is my shepherd; I shall not want" (Ps. 23:1).

The words I had spoken were images formed in me by constantly saying what God said about me!

By the time the abstracts were brought up to date for the final close, I had sold 40 acres to the school district to build a new school. It worked out to where at the final closing of the transaction, I had several thousand dollars equity in the farm, and I had not put one cent into it.

It was not what I had done.

It was God honoring faith-filled words.

Now, we come to the real reason I shared this story in this book. At the final signing of the papers, they told me that they never intended to sell the farm. Some of the heirs wanted their money, so one of the family said, "Find out what it is worth, and I will buy it and keep it in the family."

The farm had been in the family for nearly 100 years. They put it on the market, only to find out how much it was worth. They had no idea the farm was worth as much as I offered. They could take the money to the bank and draw twice as much interest as the farm was paying rent. They said, *"We would be foolish not to sell it at that price."*

It was a good deal for them and for me, for within two years the farm prices almost doubled. The thing that *turned me on* was when I realized that the farm really was not even for sale until the day that faith rose up in my spirit and caused my tongue to form the image the Word of God had painted on the inside of me. *"I will buy the farm. The farm is mine."*

Oh, thank God for the power of His Word to produce faith. *A prayer of faith set in motion had brought the opportunity before me.* But it had no real substance until I was willing to mix *faith-filled words with it.* Then, and then only did it become a reality. *Faith was the substance.*

Sometimes people say, "I have tried that and it didn't work for me. Why did it work for you?" The Word of God is the reason.

I CHOSE TO BELIEVE WHAT THE WORD SAYS ABOUT ME. Now it wasn't because I was smart. A year before I would have blown the whole deal by the words of my mouth. It wasn't because of my ability. It was simply because I programmed my heart with the Word and acted like it was true. Jesus said the good things of God come out of your heart.

"Keep thy heart with all diligence; for out of it are the issues (forces) of life" (Prov. 4:23).

In Matthew 12:35 Jesus said, **"...an evil man out of the evil treasure of his heart bringeth forth evil things."** If you want to know the evil things He's talking about, the 13th chapter of Numbers tells us what God called an *evil report. The spies were sent in to spy out the land, and ten of them came back and gave an evil report. They told what they saw, what they heard, and what they felt.*

Now what was so evil about that?

The fact that what they heard, saw, and felt was exactly contrary to what God had said.

God said, "I've given you the land." They were to go over there and plan their strategy; plan how they would take it.

They were not to go over there and see if they could take it. They were to go there and decide how they were going to do it.

They came back and said, "Whoo! There are giants over there. We were grasshoppers in their sight!"

Well, thank God! If faith will move a mountain, it'll whittle a giant down to size.

God said the things they saw, the things they heard, and the things they felt were an evil report.

We have all done it. We have gone to God and given Him an evil report. We have said in our prayer, "It didn't work, Lord. It's getting worse. I prayed and it didn't work out."

What makes you think it didn't work out?

We will say, "Well, you see, it looks worse, and I feel like things are getting worse."

That's an evil report.

You are not to be moved by what you see or feel. Be moved by WHAT THE WORD SAYS. Say only WHAT THE WORD SAYS. THE WORD says IT WILL WORK OUT. Stand on that.

STAND

The Bible says, "...and having done all, to stand. Stand therefore..." (Eph. 6:13,14).

It didn't say turn and run. It didn't say give up and say, "Dear Lord, it's not working."

It says, "WHEN YOU'VE DONE ALL to stand — STAND!" JUST STAND THERE!

"You mean, don't do anything?"

Yeah! That's what I mean. *JUST STAND THERE.*

Somebody said, "What'll I do? I prayed and it's just not working out."

Well, the first thing to do is *SHUT YOUR MOUTH.*

Second, just STAND THERE. If you can't say something good, don't say anything. It'll work out, if you have believed God.

CHAPTER 6

WATCH
YOUR WORDS

A lot of times we have *gotten off faith* and *cast out God's Words,* and started *believing what the devil said.* You release the ability of Satan when you start saying what he said.

Fear activates the devil.

Faith brings God on the scene.

Before you ever make a confession of what comes into your head, ask yourself, *"Who said that? What is its source?"*

If it doesn't agree with the *WORD,* you know who said that. The devil said it. *Don't you quote it.* If you do, that's his deception.

Did you know the devil doesn't have any power over the believer?

The only ability Satan can exercise over you is the *ability to deceive you.* If he can get you to believe his lies, he's got you playing right into his hand. And if you go quoting what he said, brother, he can put it on you stiff and strong, and all your praying won't help you *ANY.*

You can see that you've moved God out of it. You have said, *"Lord, it's getting worse —it's not getting any better." You have stopped God's ability immediately.* Maybe it was just about to come into manifestation, but now you have established Satan's word in the earth —that it's not getting any better, it's getting worse. *YOU have established his word.*

God's Word says, **"For ever, O Lord, thy word is settled in heaven"** (Ps. 119:89). God's Word is already settled in heaven.

The *WORD* says, "I will give unto thee the keys of the kingdom of heaven: and whatsoever thou shalt bind on earth shall be bound in heaven: and whatsoever thou shalt loose on earth shall be loosed in heaven" (Matt. 16:19). *He didn't say key to the kingdom. He said keys OF the kingdom.*

"Whatsoever thou shalt *bind on earth* shall be *bound in heaven:* and whatsoever thou shalt *loose on earth* shall be *loosed in heaven.*"

The Spirit of God spoke to me one morning, and He said, "The problem with the church today is that most of them are binding their finances. They are binding their spiritual growth by saying, 'The devil's hindering me. The devil just won't let me do what I want to do.'"

Well, don't ask him! Don't ask the devil about it. Go ahead and do it. You see, sometimes we've kind of buddied up with him and communicated with him, and he's told us, "Oh, you can't do that." Then we speak it out of our own mouth, "The devil's been hindering me all week. I just can't get anything done."

I have heard them say, "He's so smart. He will just put *one over on* you before you know it, and he'll just come and *foul things up* before you even know it."

Well, you have released the ability of Satan to come in and put it over on you. You have said with your mouth, "He comes up behind me when I don't know it, and he just fouls the works up."

Now, if God came in and stopped that, He would have to violate His Word because He said you can have what you say. And you have said, "Satan's smarter than I am," and he comes in, and *you* have indicated that Satan's smarter than God, and he's more powerful than God. *You don't have any Scripture for that.*

FAITH IS THE VICTORY

You do have plenty of Scripture that says God is more powerful than the devil and *He will put you over every time you act on the WORD.*

World overcoming faith dwelleth on the inside of you! **"...This is the victory that overcometh the world, even our faith"** (1 John 5:4).

So, you have a lot of Scripture to back you up in that, but you don't have any to back you up that Satan's smarter than God or smarter than you. *When you are in Christ, you have access to the mind of Christ.*

Satan is not all that smart. Can you imagine a fellow still fighting when he's already whipped? Now that's pretty stupid!

If you don't believe we have already won— go ahead — read the back of the book. "Ye are of God, little children, and have overcome them: because greater is he that is in you, than he that is in the world" (1 John 4:4). Revelation 12:11 says, "And they overcame him by the blood of the Lamb, and by the word of their testimony...."

By what? The blood of Jesus and the WORD of THEIR testimony. The word of their mouth. Did you notice that word "overcame"? The back of the book says that YOU WON, PRAISE GOD! Establish that, and quit agreeing with the devil. Quit prolonging agony.

Get in this thing and agree with what God said. You have already won. It's not your fight. Jesus fought it for you, and thank God He won! You can see that. **"For whatsoever is born of God overcometh the world."** Praise the Name of the Lord!

AUTHORITY OF WORDS

Let's go back to the 12th chapter of Matthew and look at verse 36. Jesus is speaking now. Nobody spoke with more authority than Jesus. Thank God, when Jesus spoke,

He meant it. *He meant what He said, and He said what He meant.* He never talked any foolishness. He said, **"But I say unto you, That every idle word that men shall speak, they shall give account thereof in the day of judgment."** That word *"idle"* means *non-effective* or *non-working* word. He said that every word you speak that is not working for you *will have to be accounted for by you,* in the day of Judgment.

Now when I saw that, I said, "I'm going to start watching my words." I had been saying plenty of those *idle words,* and they were not working for me. *They were working against me, not for me.*

He said if they are not working for you, you will give account for them.

Somebody said, "Well now, how's that going to be?"

Well, some folks are going to come to the judgment seat of Christ; there they are about to get their reward, and the Lord is going to say, "Now look, here's what you could have had."

"Whoo! Praise the Lord!"

Then He says, "But here's what you get."

"Uhh."

Have you ever wondered where those tears are going to come from that He said He would *wipe away?*

You saw what you could have had, and then you saw what you are getting.

You are going to say, "Oh, but Lord, I couldn't have done all that."

He will say, "See, if you had given to this missionary, souls could have been saved."

"Oh, but Lord, I didn't have the money. I didn't have it to give. I was not able to do this. I was not able to give as I wanted to. I couldn't get my hands on enough to give any away."

He will say, "That's the same problem you were having on earth. *You were agreeing with the devil.* It's true, you didn't have the money in your possession."

Then He will show you someone else and say, "Here's a man who didn't have the money, either. But he said, 'My God supplieth all my need according to his riches in glory; therefore I confess I have abundance. There is no lack. I have all sufficiency of all things. The *WORD says 'I do.'* I thank You, Father, for it. Therefore, I give it in faith and, Father, You will cause it to come to me in the Name of Jesus.' He got what he said, and here's his reward. He used his words wisely." He will say, "If you would have said what I said, if you had agreed with what I said, you could have had the better reward. But you said what the devil said. You didn't lose your soul, but you lost your reward."

JUSTIFIED OR CONDEMNED BY YOUR WORDS

You can see that the words work for or against you. He said you are going to be *justified* or *condemned* by the *words of your mouth*.

Matthew 12:37 says, "For by thy words thou shalt be justified, and by thy words thou shalt be condemned."

Actually, He's not talking about condemning you to hell. He's talking about things you can have in this life on earth and rewards of heaven.

We need to watch what we say, to set a watch on our mouth.

In the third chapter of Romans, verses 3 and 4, the Word says, "For what if some did not believe? shall their unbelief make the faith of God without effect? God forbid: yea, let God be true, but every man a liar; as it is written, *That thou mightest be justified in thy sayings, and mightest overcome when thou art judged.*"

In other words, He said that if somebody comes up with that old *unbelief* dripping off them *like molasses off a syrup bucket,* saying, "Oh, I don't believe it's going to work this time," let God be true and that man a liar. **"That thou mightest be justified in thy sayings, and mightest overcome when thou art judged."**

When you get to heaven you are going to be judged on who you believe — God or man.

Man says, "It's getting worse, you can't do that." And I tell you, it's not just the world that says that. There are some Christians that I think sometimes they have been *sprinkled with fear*, rolled in doubt, stuffed with unbelief, and insulated to the WORD OF GOD. They will believe everything but the Word of God. *Some will swallow the enemy's biggest lie, but won't believe God's simplest truth.*

They will say, "Oh yes, brother, I know that's in the Bible, but you don't understand."

Yes, I do understand. The *WORD SAYS IT WORKS,* and they are saying it won't.

"You just don't understand. I still hurt."

But, the WORD SAYS YOU'RE HEALED!

Don't misunderstand what I'm saying. I do not deny that pain exists, nor do I deny the existence of disease, but I do deny its right to continue in my body. *Feelings change. The Word does not change. If you do not feel healed, go to the Word and get you some feelings. The Word of God in your spirit will change your physical feelings.*

THE WORD BRINGS HEALTH

Proverbs 4:22 says, "...my word... is health (medicine) to all our flesh." The Word will bring health to the physical body (paraphrase).

The question is, "If some didn't believe what you said concerning healing for your body or financial needs met, would that unbelief stop the God kind of faith *(THE FAITH THAT SPEAKS)* from working?"

God forbid that ever from happening. Let men be liars, but allow God's Word to be proven true. Notice He said for *YOU TO ALLOW* the Word to become truly manifested. Thank God! **"That thou mayest be justified in thy sayings."**

CONFESSION OF THE WORD

In Matthew 10:32 it says, "Whosoever therefore shall confess me before men, him will I confess also before my Father which is in heaven."

Now what did He say?

He said, "Those who will confess me before men, I'll confess before the Father, which is in heaven."

"In the beginning was the Word, and the Word was with God, and the Word was God" (John 1:1). *Jesus and His Word are the same. You cannot separate them.* He implies that if you are confessing Jesus, you are confessing the Word. *He is the LIVING WORD OF GOD.* He said,

"If you confess my Word before men, I'll confess you before the Father."

In the Greek it could have been read this way, "...then I will give you an audience with the Father." Praise God!

In 1 John 5:15 John said, **"And if we know that he hears us, whatsoever we ask, we know that we have the petitions that we desired of Him."** In other words, if you get an audience with the Father, you will get your prayer answered, and Jesus said, "If you confess me before men," confess my WORD before men, He said that will get you an audience before the Father.

Sometimes we have confessed, "I don't know what to do. That won't work. I don't believe that's going to work out." Then we have prayed about it, *believing in unbelief,* and you didn't get an audience with the Father.

Did you know you can believe in unbelief?

Some people actually have faith in unbelief. That is what you are doing when you say "I can't do what the Word says I can do."

Here is an example. The *WORD* says, *"He that is born of God overcometh the world. You have overcome because the greater one is in you."* Now, if you deny that, you are in unbelief and have released faith in a negative statement, "But I can't. I am not able."

Jesus said, "But whosoever shall deny me before men, him will I also deny before my Father which is in heaven" (Matt. 10:33). He said, "I'll deny you."

Jesus is the *go-between.* You can see that. *He is making intercession for us.* He is the **"...High Priest of our profession** (confession), **Christ Jesus"** (Hebrews 3:1). That means that *Jesus confesses to the Father what we say as long as it agrees with the Word.* In other words, He said, "If you confess my Word before men, I'll confess what you say before the Father. You will get an audience before the Father." He said, *"What you pray that agrees with the Word, I'll see to it that it gets to the Father. You will have an audience with Him.* Then you will get your prayer answered. But if you don't do it, I'll deny you before the Father. It won't be transferred or transmitted to Him."

When you start praying and say, "Lord, I prayed and it's not working out," that is a statement of unbelief, and you have released faith in that unbelief. Jesus will not go to His

Father and say, "Father he's prayed, but it's not working out for him."

That's against the Word of God. Can you see that? He will deny that statement before the Father. When you pray that way, your prayer never gets to heaven. You can forget it. It's not going to get there.

GOD'S WORD IS WISDOM

We find in Proverbs that there are some things that we have *stumbled over* and have not *looked upon* because they are in the Old Testament. You see, a lot of times people say, "Well, you know the Old Testament is just history." But Solomon, the wisest man who ever lived until Jesus, wrote these Proverbs. **"My son, attend to my words; incline thine ear unto my sayings. Let them not depart from thine eyes; keep them in the midst of thine heart. For they are life unto those that find them, and health to all their flesh. Keep thy heart with all diligence; for out of it are the issues of life"** (Prov. 4:20-23). Keep your spirit or your heart with ALL diligence, for the forces of life come from the heart.

The word *"heart"* refers to the center of man's being, which is his *spirit.*

Here the writer of Proverbs, inspired of the Holy Spirit, is saying the same thing that Jesus said. "The good things come out of your heart," or out of your spirit.

Verse 24 says, **"Put away from thee a froward mouth, and perverse lips put far from thee,"** or speaking contrary to what the Word says, for the *WORD IS THE WISDOM OF GOD.*

GOD'S WORD IS HIS WISDOM (1 Cor. 1:30).

When we speak contrary to His Word and say, "It's not working out. I prayed, but it's not working out," that's *perverse speech.* That is *against* the Word of God.

WATCH YOUR LANGUAGE

"Thou art snared with the words of thy mouth..." **(Prov. 6:2).** Understand this — *WORDS WORK.* They will work for you just as they worked for Jesus. They are working *FOR* you or against you, whether you realize it or not.

Let me show you something before we go any further, how the words that you say are working. I've had people come in the prayer line and say, "I'm just so nervous. I don't know why I'm so nervous." I'll guarantee you, if you'd been in their home, you would have heard most of them say no less than ten times that day, "Those kids make me so nervous they just drive me up the wall."

Jesus said you *can have* what you say.

We have programmed our vocabulary with the devil's language. We have brought sickness and disease into our vocabulary, and even death. The main word so many people use to express themselves is death — the word *"death."*

"I'm just dying to do that." They will say, "I'm going to die if I don't. That just tickled me to death."

Now that, my friend, is *perverse speech.* That is contrary to God's Word. *Death is of the devil.* "Forasmuch then as the children are partakers of flesh and blood, he also himself likewise took part of the same; that through death he might destroy him that had the power of death, *that is, the devil"* (Heb. 2:14). "And death and hell were cast into the lake of fire. This is the second death" (Rev. 20:14). We need not *buddy-up* with death. All men are going to die soon enough, so don't start *buddying up* with it now.

Adam was smarter than that. It took the devil over 900 years to kill him, but now the devil has programmed his language into the human race, until people can kill themselves in about 70 years or less, by speaking his words.

When we say, "That tickled me to death," that is contrary to the Word of God.

We need to notice what the Word says about the mouth and the tongue. "The mouth of a righteous man is a well of life..." (Prov. 10:11). Verses 21 and 24 say, "The lips of the righteous feed many: but fools die for want of wisdom. The fear of the wicked, it shall come upon him: but the desire of the righteous shall be granted." The thing you fear will come upon you. Fear will activate Satan.

Job activated Satan by his fear. "...the thing which I greatly feared is come upon me..." (Job 3:25).

Active faith in the Word brings God on the scene.

Fear brings Satan on the scene.

"The mouth of the just bringeth forth wisdom: but the froward tongue shall be cut out. The lips of the righteous know what is acceptable..." (Prov. 10:31,32).

The lips of the RIGHTEOUS.

They know what is acceptable.

What is acceptable in our speech?

What God said. In fact, you'll find that when you begin to quote what God said, it's just as though God said it. If you said it in faith, it's coming out of your heart. It's just as if God said it. It will work for you just like it worked for Him; if you program your spirit with the Word of God, and believe, and doubt not in your heart. But believe that those things which you are saying will come to pass. *You see there is more to it than just saying it. The words must originate from the inner man where spiritual power is released through words.*

Now notice with me in Proverbs 11:11, **"By the blessing of the upright the city is exalted: but it is overthrown by the mouth of the wicked."** The wicked have talked against our nation, and I'll tell you a lot of Christians have done the same thing. They have said, "Ah, that bunch of *idiots* up there, they don't know what they're doing."

They should have been saying, "Thank God, I believe God to give those men in Washington the wisdom of God to deal wisely with the affairs of our nation."

If Christians would do that, it would change the situation in Washington.

Some Christians have started doing that. Really that's already happening to some degree. God has started cleaning out some problem areas in our government. God has been brought on the scene because of *faith-filled words.*

Start saying, "I thank God that the leaders of our nation have the wisdom of God." Pray for them daily. "Father, give them the wisdom of God to deal wisely with the affairs of life."

"The words of the wicked are to lie in wait for blood: but the mouth of the upright shall deliver them" (Prov. 12:6).

What will deliver them?

The mouth of the upright.

Deliverance is as close as your mouth.

The mouth contains the tongue that controls faith and fear.

Words produce after their kind.

We need to understand this. When we start speaking what God said, the devil is going to sit up and take notice.

God said to Joshua, "This book of the law shall not depart out of thy mouth; but thou shalt meditate therein day and night, *THAT thou mayest observe to do according* to all that is written therein; for *then thou shalt make thy way prosperous, and then thou shalt have good success*" (Josh. 1:8).

Who's going to do it?

We have always thought God was going to do it.

God said, "If you will do My Word, you have done it. And I'll see that it's performed."

You can see that.

I've prayed, "Father, You make this prosper," *but I was not doing the Word.* God said, "You do my Word, and it will prosper." He said, "You have made your way prosperous."

CHOOSE WORDS OF LIFE

"A man shall be satisfied with good by the fruit of his mouth..." (Prov. 12:14). The fruit of his mouth would be what his mouth produced. In other words, by the produce of his mouth, he will be satisfied or disappointed. *The words of his mouth should cause him to be satisfied with good.* Verse 17 of the same chapter says, **"He that speaketh truth sheweth forth righteousness...."**

What is truth?

THE WORD OF GOD IS TRUTH, and it *sheweth forth righteousness.* "There is that speaketh like the piercings of a sword: but the tongue of the wise is health" (Prov. 12:18).

Now you better get this one. This is stout! He said there are people speaking and it's just like jabbing a sword in you, and cutting you, and damaging you, or damaging themselves. They are desiring something from God, but they are cutting themselves up spiritually by saying, "Oh, I'm so unworthy. I can't get my prayers answered. I don't know why the Lord won't heal me." *These are people who are believers, using their tongues to destroy their faith; using their God-given ability to hold themselves in bondage.*

God gave you the ability to use your tongue to create a better life by speaking words that are full of faith. The choice is yours, whether you will speak them or not.

"And the Lord thy God will make thee plenteous in every work of thine hand, in the fruit of thy body, and in the fruit of thy cattle, and in the fruit of thy land, for good: for the Lord will again rejoice over thee for good, as he rejoiced over thy fathers:

"If thou shalt hearken unto the voice of the Lord thy God, to keep his commandments and his statutes which are written in this book of the law, and if thou turn unto the Lord thy God with all thine heart, and with all thy soul.

"For this commandment which I command thee this day, it is not hidden from thee, neither is it far off.

"It is not in heaven, that thou shouldest say, Who shall go up for us to heaven, and bring it unto us, that we may hear it, and do it?

"Neither is it beyond the sea, that thou shouldest say, Who shall go over the sea for us, and bring it unto us, that we may hear it, and do it.

"But the word is very nigh unto thee, in thy mouth, and in thy heart, that thou mayest do it.

"See, I have set before thee this day life and good, and death and evil;

"In that I command thee this day to love the Lord thy God, to walk in his ways, and to keep his commandments and his statutes and his judgments, that thou mayest live and multiply: and the Lord thy God shall bless thee in the land whither thou goest to possess it.

"But if thine heart turn away, so that thou wilt not hear, but shalt be drawn away, and worship other gods, and serve them;

"I denounce unto you this day, that ye shall surely perish, and that ye shall not prolong your days upon the land, whither thou passest over Jordan to go to possess it.

"I call heaven and earth to record this day against you, that I have set before you life and death, blessing and cursing: therefore choose life, that both thou and thy seed may live" (Deut. 30:9-19).

THE TONGUE OF THE WISE

"But the tongue of the wise is health." Praise God, *the wise talk health! They talk life! They talk healing!* **"There shall no evil happen to the just: but the wicked shall be filled with mischief"** (Prov. 12:21). The just know what is acceptable. They speak *God's Word* concerning their deliverance.

"Let the redeemed of the Lord say so, whom he hath redeemed from the hand of the enemy" (Ps. 107:2).

They speak God's Word in the face of apparent defeat. **"And the God of peace shall bruise Satan under your feet shortly..."** (Rom. 16:20).

"A man shall eat good by the fruit of his mouth..." (Prov. 13:2). The Word said it will even change your grocery basket. He shall live good by the fruit of his mouth.

"Shall" is one of the strongest words in the English language. *"Shall"* doesn't mean maybe or sometimes.

Have you ever said this? "Oh, we just can't afford that. I can't make the money last to the end of the month. We can't afford the things we need."

Jesus said He came that you might have abundance.

Some have said, "Yeah, but you don't understand. I don't have any money."

That is beside the point. Jesus said, "The thief cometh not, but for to steal, and to kill, and to destroy: I am come that they might have life, and that they might have it more abundantly" (John 10:10). The *thief comes to steal your finances, kill your faith, and destroy your health. Jesus came to undo the work of the devil.* First John 3:8 says, "...For this purpose the Son of God was manifested, that he might *DESTROY* the *works* of the devil." The literal Greek reads, "That he might *UNDO* the *works* of the devil."

Galatians 3:13-14 tells us, "Christ *HATH* redeemed us from the curse of the law, being made a curse for us...That the blessing of Abraham might come on the Gentiles through Jesus Christ...."

We find in Deuteronomy, chapters 28-30, that the curse of the law is three-fold: poverty, sickness, and spiritual death. Poverty was part of the curse and Christ redeemed us from it. Now, you may not feel like you are redeemed from poverty; you may not even look like you are, but again, that is beside the point. *The WORD says you are. Be smart enough to agree with God,* and don't quote what the devil said.

If God said I ought to have abundance, then I'm going to agree with Him. "Beloved, I wish above all things that thou mayest prosper and be in health, even as thy soul prospereth" (3 John 2).

Now whether I ever get it or not, that's up to God. As long as I say what He said and do what He said to do, I'm doing my part, and you can rest assured God will do His part. *Now, I didn't say, "Go out and write hot checks." I did not say, "Live above your means." I am saying, "Speak God's Word until it brings your means up to where you desire to live."*

Now let's read in the New Testament, starting in James 1:22-26:

"But be ye doers of the word, and not hearers only, deceiving your own selves.

"For if any be a hearer of the word, and not a doer, he is like unto a man beholding his natural face in a glass:

"For he beholdeth himself, and goeth his way, and straightway forgetteth what manner of man he was.

"But whoso looketh into the perfect law of liberty, and continueth therein, he being not a forgetful hearer, but a doer of the work, this man shall be blessed in his deed.

"If any man among you seem to be religious, and bridleth not his tongue, but deceiveth his own heart, this man's religion is vain."

A lot of folks seem religious, they even have a religious tone of voice, but the WORD says, if he doesn't control his tongue, it will destroy all that he said he believed.

You can say you believe the Bible, but if you don't control your tongue, it will cause the Word to become ineffective, as far as you are concerned. *It will be just as though it didn't exist.* The devil will come in *roughshod* and *trample* you in the dust, as long as he *controls your words.*

You need to know what the Word of God says about you.

Determine now to know what the New Covenant (contract) says about you.

Start saying what the WORD says, if you want to walk in life and health.

Confess it now, "God will perfect that which concerneth me."

ANY MAN THAT SEEMETH TO BE RELIGIOUS, AND DOESN'T BRIDLE HIS TONGUE, HE DECEIVETH HIS OWN HEART AND THAT MAN'S RELIGION IS VAIN (EMPTY).

WATCH YOUR WORDS.

CHOOSE WORDS OF LIFE AND HEALTH.

CHAPTER 7

GOD'S WORD
IS TRUTH

F or what if some did not believe? shall their unbelief make the faith of God without effect? God forbid: yea, let God be true, but every man a liar..." (Rom. 3:3,4).

Proverbs 13:13 says, **"Whoso despiseth the word shall be destroyed...,"** shall be destroyed because he has rejected TRUTH.

TRUTH IS THE STABILIZING FORCE OF LIFE.

The Word of God is TRUTH. Jesus said, "...If ye continue in my word, then are ye my disciples indeed: And ye shall know the truth, and the truth shall make you free" (John 8:31,32). Jesus also said in John 6:63, "...the words that I speak unto you, they are spirit, and they are life." Jesus spoke Spirit words and they became stabilizing forces of life. Jesus spoke only that which He heard the Father say. He said in John 5:30, "I can of mine own self do nothing: as I hear, I judge: and my judgment is just; because I seek not mine own will, but the will of the Father which hath sent me."

Jesus spoke God's Word continually. He was established in His Father's Word. He overcame the world, the flesh, and the devil by the spoken Word. **"These things I have spoken unto you, that in me ye might have peace. In the world ye shall have tribulation: but be of good cheer; I have overcome the world"** (John 16:33). Matthew chapter 4, verses 4, 7, and 10, tell us that the only thing that Jesus used against the devil was the SPOKEN WORD. He spoke the written Word. IT IS WRITTEN. Oh, thank God it is still WRITTEN today. However, in book form, the Word has no power until read or spoken by someone.

In Luke's Gospel, chapter 6, beginning with verse 46, "And why call ye me, Lord, Lord, and do not the things which I say?" Verse 47, "Whosoever cometh to me, and heareth my sayings, and doeth them, I will shew you to whom he is like." Now Jesus is about to tell you how important it is to practice the Word, or to be a performer of the Word. Verse 48, "He is like a man which built an house, and digged deep, and laid the foundation on a rock: and when the flood arose, the stream beat vehemently upon that house, and could not shake it: for it was founded upon a rock."

Notice, this man dug deep and started building his foundation on something that was already established and was unshakable. *THAT IS THE WORD OF GOD. His life* was based upon God's Word.

Although they beat upon him, the flood and stream could not shake him.

Circumstances won't shake a man who believes the Word. Psalm 112:7 tells us, "He shall not be afraid of evil tidings: his heart is fixed, trusting in the Lord."

However, Luke, chapter 6, verse 49, says, "But he that heareth, and doeth not, is like a man that without a foundation built an house upon the earth; against which the stream did beat vehemently, and immediately it fell; and the ruin of that house was great."

What caused this man to be defeated in life?

It was not the flood or stream. Actually, they had nothing to do with the destruction. He heard the same Word, but his life was not based upon the Word. He did not do the Word. He suffered great loss needlessly.

Notice it didn't say one was saved and the other was not. The indication is that both came unto Him and both heard what He said.

Today many are born again and hear the Word, but hearing the Word is not the foundation spoken of in the above verses. *Doing the Word is the foundation that made this man successful in life.*

"My people are destroyed for lack of knowledge: because thou hast rejected knowledge, I will also reject thee..." (Hos. 4:6). God's Word is the only TRUE KNOWLEDGE. *It will make you stable even in the storms of life.*

Speaking God's Word will bring God on the scene. **"I am watching over my word to perform it"** (Jer. 1:12, Amplified version).

To despise, reject, or even disagree with the Word opens the door to Satan. *If you despise the Word, you have invited destruction.*

"A good man leaveth an inheritance to his children's children: and the wealth of the sinner is laid up for the just" (Prov. 13:22).

Have you ever read that scripture before?

"...the wealth of the sinner is laid up for the just." And it is beginning to change hands. When you and I begin to act on the Word of God, when we get our speech in line with the Word, we will see God move in our behalf.

We have said, "Oh, it looks like the wicked prosper."

Well, we said they were. That is one reason they are prospering.

You have said, "Oh, they can do just anything, and whatever they do will prosper."

You have been releasing faith to prosper the wicked. The words of the believer are powerful when spoken in faith.

Jesus said nothing shall be impossible to him that believeth.

Too many times we have had more faith that the wicked would prosper than we did in God's Word to put us over. And that's totally unscriptural.

We read in Isaiah 54, verses 14 and 15, "In righteousness shalt thou be established: thou shalt be far from oppression; for thou shalt not fear: and from terror; for it shall not come near thee. Behold, they shall surely gather together, but not by me: whosoever shall gather together against thee shall fall for thy sake." Now, let's go down to verse 17, "No weapon that is formed against thee shall prosper; and every tongue that shall rise against thee in judgment thou shalt condemn. This is the heritage of the servants of the Lord, and their righteousness is of me, saith the Lord."

Make this your confession, "NO WEAPON FORMED AGAINST ME SHALL PROSPER."

"Blessed is the man that walketh not in the counsel of the ungodly, nor standeth in the way of sinners, nor sitteth in the seat of the scornful.

"But his delight is in the law of the Lord; and in his law doth he meditate day and night.

"And he shall be like a tree planted by the rivers of water, that bringeth forth his fruit in his season; his leaf also shall not wither; and whatsoever he doeth shall prosper" (Ps. 1:1-3).

Notice the Word said, WHATSOEVER YOU DO SHALL PROSPER. It did not say whatsoever the wicked doeth. Verses 4 and 5 of the same chapter say, **"The ungodly are not so: but are like the chaff which the wind driveth away. Therefore the ungodly shall not stand in the judgment, nor sinners in the congregation of the righteous."** So, you can see that *it is against the Word of God to say the wicked prosper and I suffer need.*

Learn to put the WORD into confession form. Confess this before you go any further in this book, "NO WEAPON FORMED AGAINST ME WILL PROSPER, BUT WHATSOEVER I DO WILL PROSPER." Say it again, aloud.

Let these words penetrate your spirit. "MY GOD SUPPLIETH ALL MY NEED ACCORDING TO HIS RICHES IN GLORY BY CHRIST JESUS" (Phil. 4:19).

START AGREEING
WITH THE WORD

Start agreeing with the Word that your prosperity is sure, physically, spiritually, and financially. The third epistle of John verse 2 says, "Beloved, I wish above all things that thou mayest prosper and be in health, even as thy soul prospereth."

Now don't start praying that the wicked will lose everything they have. That will get you in trouble.

Just start confessing, "Thank God, the wealth of the sinner is laid up for the just. I thank God, I am the just, and I will get my part by acting on the Word."

They haven't acted on the Word, and God said that the wicked shall be cut off. Their name will rot, and they shall not be found.

Notice in Proverbs, chapter 14, verse 3, "In the mouth of the foolish is a rod of pride: but the lips of the wise shall preserve them."

The lips of the wise WILL preserve him. They WILL preserve him through financial crisis. They WILL preserve him when they say there's a recession or a depression. His lips WILL preserve him if he confesses what the WORD SAYS: if he acts on the Word.

CREATIVE ABILITY

"The tongue of the wise useth knowledge aright..." (Prov. 15:2). The knowledge that we have, we are to use it aright. THE TONGUE of the wise use knowledge. It is the tongue that makes good use of knowledge. **"A wholesome tongue is a tree of life..."** (Prov. 15:4). A wholesome tongue will bring healing as a tree of life. The wholesome TONGUE has creative ability.

Now, down to verse 13. "A merry heart maketh a cheerful countenance: but by sorrow of the heart the spirit is broken."

I've seen people come in the prayer line and just start bawling and squawling, "Oh dear God, I want to be healed. Please heal me, please heal me."

I've stopped them sometimes and said, "Now, wait a minute, get a smile on your face, because we are going to pray and God will heal you. Now why would you be brokenhearted?"

You see, the real reason people beg is they don't believe that they will receive if they ask. Many of the tears shed in prayer lines are tears of self-pity. Self-pity in a prayer line adds up to one thing: faith in the devil's ability to make sickness and disease lord over you.

I was in Dallas, Texas, in January 1975 in a certain meeting, and the Word of the Lord came unto me saying, "Tears of self-pity are a subtle form of unbelief. *Do not be deceived by them. Turn to My Word. Lean heavily upon it. Then you will learn to release your faith in laughter.* Then, you will surely turn to the enemy in the face of adversity and say, 'Ha, ha, ha, ha, ha, ha, ha.'"

The Word said, **"By sorrow of the heart the spirit is broken."** And we have prayed a lot of the time, "Oh Lord, just break me — break me."

He doesn't want you broken.

He wants you acting on the Word.

Now notice in verse 15, "All the days of the afflicted are evil: but he that is of a merry heart hath a continual feast."

Oh, thank God! "He that is of a merry heart hath a continual feast." Then, I didn't laugh until I thought I'd die; I laughed until I knew I would live forever, and have a feast while I'm doing it!

The Word says He will prepare a table before you in the presence of your enemies (Ps. 23:5).

Someone said, "Oh, when we get to heaven we're going to sit at that banquet table."

Well, there won't be any enemies in heaven! *It's here on earth he's talking about.* Most Christians have put it off until the afterlife. Oh, praise God! You can have it NOW! Here on this earth!

In fact, I'm convinced the only thing that you can't have here on this earth is the glorified body. You can have the kingdom and the benefits of it right here on this earth. The Bible says, **"It is your Father's good pleasure to give you the kingdom"** (Luke 12:32). The literal Greek says, "The Father took delight in giving you the kingdom." *The kingdom of God is in you. Now the good things come out of the heart.*

Where is the kingdom?

It's in the heart. The good things come out of the heart.... **"out of the abundance of the heart the mouth**

speaketh" (Matt. 12:34). That is the way the good things come out, in word form, spoken words.

WORDS ARE YOUR ABILITY

It is in your power to release the ability of God. Start saying, "The power of God is in me to put me over." "Greater is he that's within me than he that is in the world" (1 John 4:4). "I'm quickened according to the Word of God. *I thank God that the ABILITY OF GOD IS RELEASED WITHIN ME.* I stand before demons, I stand before sickness and disease, and I have no fear, because the ABILITY OF GOD IS RELEASED WITHIN ME, by the words of my mouth and by the WORD OF GOD. Praise the name of the Lord!"

In Proverbs, chapter 15, verse 23, it says, "A man hath joy by the answer of his mouth...."

Now you can see that. A man has joy by what he says. That is the reason folks come in the prayer line, squawling, and bawling, and pleading for God to heal them. They have said, "I don't think I'll ever get healed. I'll probably be like this the rest of my life."

They don't have any joy because of what they said. They have said, "The devil has defeated me. The devil is hindering me. The devil has done this — the devil has done that."

Forget the devil and act on the Word!

In 1 Timothy 4:1, Paul said, "Now the Spirit speaketh expressly, that in the latter times some shall depart from the faith, giving heed to seducing spirits, and doctrines of devils." Paul said they will give too much attention to the devil and his bunch.

In a certain church one Sunday, I counted the times the devil's name was mentioned. He got twice as much priority as Jesus. *Learn to write his name with a little "d."* GET YOUR SWORD! If you want to give any attention to him, get your sword and whittle up on him a while. *Put the WORD on him, and he'll leave. He won't stay around long. He can't stand the Word.* But as long as you testify for him he will buddy up with you.

"The heart of the wise teacheth his mouth, and addeth learning to his lips" (Prov. 16:23).

What WILL teach his mouth?

It didn't say God would do it. "The heart of the wise teacheth his mouth...."

Now you are back to the kingdom again, "Out of the abundance of your heart, the mouth speaketh." Then he said, **"The heart of the wise teacheth his mouth and addeth learning to his lips."**

Proverbs 16:24 says, "Pleasant words are as an honeycomb, sweet to the soul, and health to the bones."

Some folks' bones have just dried up because they have talked doubt and fear, and walked in unbelief. *They continually think about what the enemy is doing.* They say, "Oh, the devil's on a rampage today."

Some people think that the devil is alive and doing well. That's not true. He is not doing so well.

No, thank God, the devil is in trouble. He is alive, but he's not very well, I'll tell you for sure. He has knots all over his head. If you haven't put any knots there, shame on you: you should have been cutting him up with the sword, the Word of God.

Thank God, the devil is not doing well. Read the back of the book. He's losing ground every day. We should be confessing, "The enemy is losing ground every day."

We need to quit saying that the devil is doing well. Now, if you pinpoint what he's doing, it does look like he's done pretty well. Just get over here on the other side and see what God is doing. You will find that the enemy is not doing so good.

There are more people being filled with the Spirit than ever before: Catholics, Methodists, Presbyterians, all denominations, all over. There are prayer meetings going on every night, by the hundreds of thousands.

They didn't put that on TV, did they? They just put what the enemy is doing on TV.

Proverbs 18:4 says, "The words of a man's mouth are as deep waters, and the wellspring of wisdom as a flowing brook." In the Amplified version of the Bible, verse 7 says, "A fool's mouth is his ruin, and his lips are the snare to himself." Now you notice, it didn't say a "wicked" man; it said a "fool."

I'm not calling anybody a fool, but I've seen some Christian folks whose mouths were causing destruction.

Understand this, *the believer is a dangerous person.* The enemy doesn't go out and stir up sinners when he wants to cause problems in the church. *Their words don't amount to anything. They fall to the ground.*

But when you start believing WHAT YOU SAY WILL COME TO PASS, then you have creative power going for you.

That's the reason the devil wants Christians to talk negatively. It will destroy; it will tear down.

We need to get wised-up on that. You have creative power right in your mouth. Learn to release it wisely and accurately.

"For what if some did not believe? shall their unbelief make the faith of God without effect? God forbid: yea, let God be true and every man a liar..." (Rom. 3:3,4). "Whoso despiseth the Word shall be destroyed..." (Prov. 13:13).

GOD'S WORD IS TRUTH. "For the *truth's* sake, which dwelleth in us, and shall be *with us for ever*" (2 John 2).

CHAPTER 8

THE ABILITY OF THE TONGUE

The tongue has the ability to destroy you or put you over in life. Out of the same mouth comes blessing and cursing.

These things ought not to be so. The words of Jesus ring very clear: "Out of the abundance of the heart the mouth speaketh."

Your heart (spirit) is programmed by words. Faith cometh by hearing and hearing the Word of God. Fear comes by hearing what the enemy said. Many Christians have continually confessed the words of their enemy, the devil. They establish his words on earth and are held in bondage by them.

Let's think about this for a minute. No person on this earth, who is in his right mind, would go around always confessing or saying the same thing his enemies say. You can understand why you would not want to do that in the natural world. *You have enough sense to know that your enemies' words are designed to work against you.* If you were to say the same thing the enemy said about you, you might be calling yourself a liar, a thief, or a no good, unworthy sinner.

You can see the parallel. That is exactly what the enemy is trying to get you to do with your own words. He wants you to create a distorted, unworthy, self-destructive image on the inside of you (in your spirit), with words authored by the enemy of your soul.

Jesus tells us in Matthew 12:35, **"A good man out of the good treasure of the heart bringeth forth good things...."** Notice who Jesus said would cause it to be manifested. He didn't say that God would do it. Man brings it forth. Not out of his head or intellect, but out of his heart. Jesus said that the good things and bad things of life come out of the heart and they are released out of the mouth. **"Not that which goeth into the mouth defileth a man;**

but that which cometh out of the mouth, this defileth a man" (Matt. 15:11). "But those things which proceed out of the mouth come forth from the heart; and they defile the man. For out of the heart proceed evil thoughts, murders, adulteries, fornications, thefts, false witness, blasphemies" (Matt. 15:18,19).

The last thing the devil ever wants you to see is the facts of the recreated spirit. Here are some of these facts. You are created IN Christ Jesus, you are His workmanship, not your own. "For we are his workmanship, created in Christ Jesus unto good works, which God hath before ordained that we should walk in them" (Eph. 2:10). "Therefore if any man be in Christ, he is a new creature: old things are passed away; behold, all things are become new" (2 Cor. 5:17). Old things have passed away out of your spirit. All things concerning your spirit have become new. Jesus became sin that you would become the righteousness of God in Christ Jesus. "For he hath made him to be sin for us, who knew no sin; that we might be made the righteousness of God in him" (2 Cor. 5:21). You, as a born-again believer, are an heir of God, a joint-heir of Christ. "And if children, then heirs; heirs of God, and

joint-heirs with Christ; if so be that we suffer with him, that we may be also glorified together" (Rom. 8:17). You are fully able to come into the Father's presence without fear or condemnation. You are free from the law of sin that produces spiritual death. **"There is therefore now no condemnation to them which are in Christ Jesus, who walk not after the flesh, but after the Spirit. For the law of the Spirit of life in Christ Jesus hath made me free from the law of sin and death"** (Rom. 8:1,2).

You have become a son of God so you can be a partaker of His divine nature, very capable of fellowshipping with Deity.

Now Satan can't do that. He has no fellowship with Deity. He is a dead spirit; he cannot function in the realm of the God life as a man can. The reborn human spirit is a higher creation. Man was created to have fellowship with Deity.

SPIRIT WORDS

The spirit of man is not of this world. It is of the spirit world. The creative ability of man comes through this spirit.

When man has God's Word abundantly abiding in his heart and speaks it forth in faith, he speaks spirit words that work in the world of the spirit. They will also dominate the physical world. He breathes spirit life into God's Word and it becomes a living substance, working for him as it worked for God in the beginning. These Spirit Words dominate the natural world.

Jesus said, **"...the words that I speak unto you, they are spirit and they are life"** (John 6:63). They were the Words of God, received into His Spirit, and being abundantly in His Spirit (heart), He released faith in word form through the words of His mouth. *His words penetrated the spirits of men.* Their spirit heard Him and they acted from their spirit on Spirit Words. **"...take up thy bed, and walk"** *(John 5:8)*. **"...Stretch forth Thine hand"** *(Mark 3:5)*. **"...Damsel, I say unto thee, arise"** *(Mark 5:41)*. **"...Young man, I say unto thee, Arise"** *(Luke 7:14)*. **"...Lazarus, come forth"** *(John 11:43)*. The Words He spoke were truly Spirit Words, full of life.

It is that same Spirit that raised Christ from the dead. "But if the Spirit of him that raised up Jesus from the dead dwell in you, he that raised up Christ from the dead shall also quicken your mortal bodies by his Spirit that dwelleth in you" (Rom. 8:11). It does make mortal bodies alive. Spirit Words spoken by Jesus ignited the faith that was already residing in these people. It caused an explosion of God's ability on their behalf. It was all set in motion by words spoken in faith.

FAITH TO BE HEALED

I remember a few years ago, I was teaching in a Faith Seminar in Arkansas. One night a lady came forward in the prayer line to be ministered to for someone else by the laying on of hands. As I do quite often, I said to her, "Sister, raise your hands and make a faith statement of what will happen when hands are laid on you in the Name of Jesus."

She raised her hands no higher than her shoulders and said, "I can't raise them any higher than this."

I said, "Why not?"

"Because of this arthritis," she answered.

I heard the Spirit of God say, "Yes, she can in the Name of Jesus."

I just touched her on the forehead and said, "Yes, you can in the Name of Jesus."

She said, "Praise the Lord," and both hands went up over her head, instantly.

Sometimes you have to shock people into releasing their faith. *She had faith to be healed. The Spirit of God revealed that to me.* Now, if I had asked her if she had faith to be healed of that condition, she would probably have said, "No, if I did, I wouldn't have arthritis now."

Probably no one had ever told her she could raise her hands over her head. Most people agreed she couldn't. *But faith dared to speak and she believed.*

PROCLAIM MORE BOLDLY

I was in Walnut Ridge, Arkansas, one night to speak at a Full Gospel Business Men's meeting.

Before the service started someone called in a prayer request. A baby had just been born *prematurely,* and the doctor said he couldn't live. They had sent the baby on to Memphis, Tennessee, in an ambulance. The doctor had already told the family that the baby would die; he could not live.

As I heard the request I said to myself, "I bind those words in the Name of Jesus, and I say the baby will live and not die."

Then the man called on me to pray for this request. As I walked to the front, I began to realize that now we were going to find out if I really believe what I said, within myself. So, as I stood up to pray, I asked the congregation to agree with me in prayer. I prayed a simple prayer, "Father, You said in Your Word, 'whatsoever things you desire when you pray, believe that you receive them and you shall have them,' so we come in behalf of this baby who the doctor says will die. I say in the Name of Jesus the baby will live and not die. I say in the Name of Jesus that healing power flows to that baby and it will live and not die."

Now instantly my head gave me trouble; it was really the devil putting these thoughts in my mind. He said, "You are a nut. You are going to look silly because the baby is already dead." My head was screaming, "The baby is dead already."

But the Lord had spoken to me a few months before and said, "When the dry winds of doubt begin to blow, just proclaim more boldly that which you hear in your spirit." He said that was what He did at the tomb of Lazarus.

So, I said in my prayer several times, "The baby will live and not die."

Well, we had a good meeting there that night. Several people were healed.

About two or three weeks later I received a letter from the president of the Full Gospel Business Men's chapter and he told me this story. I quote, "As I left the meeting that night I went by the hospital to see the family of the child." He said, "It was the hardest thing I ever did. It took all the faith I had to tell them the baby will live and not die, but you told me to do it so I did. I told them their baby will live and not die."

When I read the letter I asked my wife if I told him to do that, because I didn't remember doing it.

She said, "No, I didn't hear you say that."

So, it must have been the Lord who spoke that into his spirit. Now I am glad the man did, but I didn't tell him to do it. The family was already resigned to accept what the doctor had said, and had already given the baby up to die. The doctor had said the baby would not live until they reached Memphis.

The baby did live and within a few days was doing fine.

About ten days later the father, who was not born again, brought the baby to church and testified to the fact that God had miraculously healed his child.

THE POWER OF FAITH-FILLED WORDS

It could have been a very different story. If we had said, "Well, if it's the Lord's will: if God doesn't undertake, he will die."

No, thank God, Jesus said, "You can have what you say."

That being true, why not learn to say what you desire, not what *seems* to exist?

Mark 11:23-24 tells us, "...he shall have whatsoever he saith. Therefore I say unto you, What things soever ye desire, when ye pray (say), believe that ye receive them, and ye shall have them."

Oh, the power of faith-filled words! I simply spoke boldly the desired results in prayer, and because it was spoken so boldly and emphatic, it caused many people to agree with my words.

Jesus said, "If two of you agree on earth...it shall be done for them by my Father."

The president of the Full Gospel chapter proved he believed it by saying it to the whole family. *He really believed it in his heart.* It was the abundance of faith in his heart that caused him to speak it forth when the family had given the child up.

When you speak more boldly, more people will agree with you.

FAITH-FILLED WORDS
SPARK OTHERS' FAITH

Faith-filled words spark others' faith that is dormant or inactive and cause it to be released. There is creative power released when you proclaim boldly things that are in agreement with the Word of God, and it causes others to release their faith.

FAITH RESIDES IN THE SPIRIT

Notice very carefully what happened in Acts 14:8-10 New Living Translation, "**While they were at Lystra, Paul and Barnabas came upon a man with crippled feet. He had been that way from birth, so he had never walked. He was sitting and listening as Paul preached. Looking straight at him, Paul realized he had faith to be healed.**

"**So Paul called to him in a loud voice, 'Stand up!' And the man jumped to his feet and started walking.**" Paul perceived by the Spirit of God that the man who was crippled had faith sufficient to bring healing. The faith was not in the physical man; it does not operate through the physical.

The words Paul spoke were creative power. They were spirit words inspired by the Spirit of God. He spoke them to the man on the inside. If he had been talking to the man's physical mind, he would have had to explain to him that he did have faith. *But the spirit man is where faith resides. Physical words would be used to speak to the physical man.* The words Paul spoke would have made no sense whatsoever to the physical intellect. Spirit words. Words filled with Spirit life. Not authored by man, authored by God. *But spoken by Paul. "STAND UPRIGHT ON THY FEET!"*

Now you realize that he is talking to the man on the inside, the spirit man. It would have been useless to tell the physical man to stand up, since he had never walked. His intellect knew physically he could not do that. If it could have been done physically by the man himself, don't you know he would not have stayed in that condition. But it was beyond his physical and mental ability.

The ability had to come from his spiritual resources, the spirit man on the inside of him. However, they were received into his spirit, *"STAND UPRIGHT ON THY FEET"* *and he LEAPED and WALKED.* Spirit words received into his spirit released spiritual power in his physical body.

This creative ability of spirit words formed in his spirit and produced physical results.

FAITH MUST BE RELEASED

In Acts 9:34, Peter spoke to a man who had been bedfast for eight years. He did not pray for him, nor did he tell him he would remember him in prayer, as we so often do. Peter spoke to the "spirit man." **"And Peter said unto him, Aeneas, Jesus Christ maketh thee whole: arise, and make thy bed. And he arose immediately."**

This was an impossible task for the physical man. But Peter's words went deeper than the physical. His tongue formed spirit words, CREATIVE POWER, that ignited faith that was pent up in the spirit man, but had never been released in action form. *"But wilt thou know, O vain man, that faith without works is dead?"* (James 2:20).

Faith that is not released into action is as gas that has not been ignited. It produces no power. In James 3:6 the Word says, "And the tongue is a fire, a world of iniquity: so is the tongue among our members, that it defileth the whole body, and setteth on fire the course of nature; and it is set on fire of hell." In other words, the tongue in the untamed state is a fire and a world of wickedness, and the fire that is in the tongue is from hell.

Natural humanity cannot tame or control this fire that is in the tongue. But oh, thank God, Jesus made provision for this tongue to be not only tamed, but also set aflame with the Holy Ghost fire. **"You shall receive power, after that the Holy Ghost is come upon you..."** (Acts 1:8). **"...he shall baptize YOU with the Holy Ghost and with FIRE"** (Luke 3:16). **"And there appeared to them tongues resembling fire, which were separated and distributed and that settled upon each one of them"** *(Acts 2:3 Amplified).* **"And they were all filled with the Holy Ghost, and began to speak with other tongues, as the Spirit gave them utterance"** *(Acts 2:4).*

NATURAL MEN BECOME SUPERNATURAL

Two marvelous things happened to the HUNDRED AND TWENTY on the day of Pentecost.

First — They were born again. "Jesus answered and said unto him, Verily, verily, I say unto thee, Except a man be born again, he cannot see the kingdom of God" (John 3:3). *Natural men became supernatural men.* Jesus said you can't put new wine in old bottles. *New wine must be put in new bottles. They became new creation men.* "Therefore if any man be in Christ, he is a new creature: old things are passed away; behold, all things are become new" (2 Cor. 5:17). *Supernatural men that never existed before in this righteous state.* "For he hath made him to be sin for us, who knew no sin; that we might be made the righteousness of God in him" (2 Cor. 5:21). They were not now sinners saved by grace, but new creations in Christ. "For we are his workmanship, created in Christ Jesus unto good works, which God hath before ordained that we should walk in them" (Eph. 2:10), *no longer totally subject to their natural ability.*

Second — They were baptized with Holy Ghost and FIRE (Luke 3:16), and spoke with other tongues as the spirit gave them utterance. The tongue that had been an unruly evil, full of deadly poison, set on fire of hell, was now set aflame of the Holy Ghost. God's Spirit had come to abide in the spirit of man. **"And I will pray the Father, and he shall give you another Comforter, that he may abide with you forever"** (John 14:16). *SUPERNATU-RAL men born of God.* **"Whosoever believeth that Jesus is the Christ is born of God: and every one that loveth him that begat loveth him also that is begotten of him. By this we know that we love the children of God, when we love God, and keep his commandments. For this is the love of God, that we keep his commandments: and his commandments are not grievous. *For whatsoever is born of God overcometh the world...even our faith"*** (1 John 5:1-4).

Men that will overcome the world and have dominion over the circumstances of life. *Men that would dare speak as God spoke. Men with tongues of fire.* Men who dare say to a man who had been hopelessly crippled for forty years, who had never walked one step in his entire life: *"In the name of Jesus Christ of Nazareth RISE UP AND WALK!...* and he leaping up stood, and walked, and entered with them into the temple, walking, and leaping, and praising God" (Acts 3:6,8). *Peter's tongue, now aflame of the Holy Spirit, had become a creative force, releasing God's ability.*

DEATH AND LIFE ARE IN THE POWER OF THE TONGUE

The words of your mouth and the meditation of your heart need to be acceptable in the sight of the Lord.

We should confess, "I let no corrupt communication proceed out of my mouth, but that which is good to edifying that it may minister grace to the hearer."

"A man's belly (innermost being) shall be satisfied with the fruit of his mouth; and with the increase of his lips shall he be filled" (Prov. 18:20). The Amplified Version of the Bible says, "A man's moral self shall be filled with the fruit of his mouth, and with the consequence of his words he must be satisfied (whether good or evil)."

Proverbs 18:21 says, **"Death and life are in the power of the tongue: and they that love it shall eat the fruit**

thereof." The Amplified Version says, "Death and life are in the power of the tongue, and they who indulge in it shall eat the fruit of it (for death or life)."

"He who guards his mouth keeps his life" (Prov. 13:3, Amplified Version).

Now, James 3:6 says this about the tongue.

It is set on fire of hell. It's full of death carrying venom.

IT CAN KILL YOU, *OR* IT CAN *RELEASE* THE LIFE OF GOD WITHIN YOU.

CHAPTER 9

GOD'S CREATIVE POWER® WILL WORK FOR YOU

THE GREAT CONFESSION

Christianity is called the *great confession,* but most Christians who are defeated in life are defeated because they believe and confess the wrong things. They have spoken the words of the enemy. And those *words* hold them in bondage. Proverbs 6:2 says, **"Thou art snared with the words of thy mouth."**

Faith-filled words will put you over.

Fear-filled words will defeat you.

Words are the most powerful thing in the universe. Their importance is seen from Genesis, **"Let us make man in our image..."** (Gen. 1:26), through Revelation, "...They overcame him by the blood of the Lamb, and by the *WORD* of their *testimony..."* (Rev. 12:11).

God created the universe with the spoken WORD. "Through faith we understand that the worlds were framed by the word of God, so that things which are seen were not made of things which do appear" (Heb. 11:3).

Genesis 1 is a copy of the words God used to release His faith. John 1:1-3 tells us that, "In the beginning was the Word, and the Word was with God, and the Word was God. The same was in the beginning with God. All things were made by him; and without him was not any thing made that was made." *It was the WORD that was with God and the WORD WAS GOD.*

One of the laws of Genesis is that every thing produces after its kind. "And God said, Let the earth bring forth grass, the herb yielding seed, and the fruit tree yielding fruit after his kind, whose seed is in itself, upon the earth: and it was so. And the earth brought forth grass, and herb yielding seed after his kind, and the tree yielding fruit, whose seed was in itself, after his kind: and God saw that it was good" (Gen. 1:11,12).

Then in Genesis 1, verse 26-28, we find three of the most astounding statements found in the Bible:

1. "Let us make man in our image, after our likeness."

2. "So God created man in His own image."

3. "Replenish the earth, and subdue it: and have dominion."

John 4:24 says, "God is a Spirit: and they that worship him must worship him in spirit and in truth."

Man was created in God's class: very capable of operating in the same kind of faith. Man is a spirit, he has a soul, and he lives in a body. Genesis 2:7 tells us God made man's body out of the dust of the earth, but plainly states, **"and breathed into his nostrils the breath of life."** That life was spirit life, the very life of God. Man is a spirit being, very capable of operating on the same level of faith as God.

We read in Mark 9:23, "Jesus said unto him, If thou canst believe, all things are possible to him that believeth." Matthew 17:20 says, "And Jesus said unto them,

...for verily I say unto you, If ye have faith as a grain of mustard seed, ye shall say unto this mountain, Remove hence to yonder place; and it shall remove; and nothing shall be impossible unto you." Mark 11:23 says, "For verily I say unto you, That whosoever shall say unto this mountain, Be thou removed, and be thou cast into the sea; and shall not doubt in his heart, but shall believe that those things which he saith shall come to pass; he shall have whatsoever he saith."

SPIRITUAL LAW

This is not theory. It is fact. *It is spiritual law.* It works every time it is applied correctly. *God never does anything without saying it first. God is a faith God. God released His faith in words.* **"And Jesus answering saith unto them, Have faith in God"** (Mark 11:22). A more literal translation of the above verse says, "Have the God kind of faith, or faith of God."

Ephesians 5:1 literally tells us to be imitators of God as children imitate their parents.

To imitate God, you must talk like Him and act like Him.

He would not ask you to do something you are not capable of doing.

Jesus operated in the faith principles of Mark 11:23 and Matthew 17:20 while He was on earth. He spoke to the wind and sea. He spoke to demons. He spoke to the fig tree. He even spoke to dead men.

The wind, sea, tree, demons, even the dead were obedient to what He said.

He operated in the God kind of faith.

God is a faith God. God released His faith in words.

Jesus was imitating His Father and getting the same results as His Father.

In John 14:12 Jesus said, "...He that believeth on me, the works that I do shall he do also; and greater...."

These principles of faith are based on spiritual laws. They work for whosoever will apply these laws.

You set them in motion by the words of your mouth. That's the way you are saved, by confessing Jesus as Lord. "That if thou shalt confess with thy mouth the Lord Jesus, and shalt believe in thine heart that God hath raised him from the dead, thou shalt be saved. For with the heart man believeth unto righteousness; and with the mouth confession is made unto salvation" (Rom. 10:9,10). Faith-filled words released out of your mouth defeated Satan and created the reality of God's Word in your spirit. Speaking God's Word after Him caused you to become a new creation that never existed before.

Jesus said, "He shall have whatsoever he saith."

It won't happen just because you say it.

You must release faith in the words you speak from the heart. You must believe that those things which you are saying will come to pass.

This law is working for or against you every day.

Do you really want all the negative things you have been confessing to come to pass? Are you believing for those things?

If Jesus came to you personally and said, from this day forward it will come to pass, that every thing you say will happen exactly as you say it, would that change your vocabulary?

I believe it would.

BINDING AND LOOSING

In Matthew 16:19 Jesus said, "I will give unto thee the keys of the kingdom of heaven: whatsoever thou shalt bind on earth will be bound in heaven: whatsoever thou shalt loose on earth shall be loosed in heaven."

Psalm 119:89 tells us, **"For ever, O Lord, thy word is settled in heaven."** What God said is already established.

Now, it is up to you.

What are you going to say about it?

God will not alter what He has said. "My covenant will I not break, nor alter the thing that is gone out of my lips" (Ps. 89:34).

Whose words will you establish on earth?

The power of binding and loosing is on earth. It is not in heaven. According to Matthew 16:19, you are the one doing the binding, and He said all heaven will stand behind what you say. Many Christians have bound their finances and loosed the enemy by the words of their mouth. They have bound their spiritual growth by confessing the enemy's ability to hinder them. They have more faith in the enemy to defeat them than they have in God to put them over. And there is no scriptural basis for that kind of belief, or should I say unbelief.

WORLD OVERCOMER

The Word says, **"...Whatsoever is born of God overcometh the world..."** (1 John 5:4). You are a world overcomer.

Confess it right now. "I AM A WORLD OVERCOMER BECAUSE I AM BORN OF GOD. I AM A WORLD OVERCOMER BECAUSE I AM BORN OF GOD." Say it again and again.

You may not feel like it. The Word didn't say you were if you felt like it.

God's Word said you were. How you feel has nothing to do with God being truthful. If He said I am a world overcomer, then thank God, that's good enough for me.

I am not a *world overcomer* because of how I feel, or how I look. I don't always feel like one. I don't always look like one, but thank God, because He says I am, I AM A WORLD OVERCOMER! I confess it daily.

It's true and I know it, but I confessed it aloud before God the Father, Jesus, the angels, before demons, and anyone else that would listen for months before I began to feel like it was true.

The feeling came only after my spirit received God's Word as the final authority.

God's Word said it — then I am whether I feel like it or not.

God cannot lie.

SPOKEN WORDS

Spoken words program your spirit (heart) either for success or defeat.

Words are containers. They carry faith or fear, and they produce after their kind.

"So then faith cometh by hearing, and hearing by the word of God" (Rom. 10:17). Faith comes more quickly when you hear yourself quoting, speaking, and saying the things God said. You will more readily receive God's Word into your spirit by hearing yourself say it than if you hear someone else say it.

LIVE IN THE AUTHORITY OF THE WORD

The Spirit of God spoke to me concerning confessing the Word of God aloud: where you can hear yourself saying it.

He said, "It is a scientific application of the wisdom of God to the psychological makeup of man."

And it works, thank God. *The body of Christ must begin to live in the authority of the Word. For God's Word is creative power.* That creative power is produced by the heart, formed by the tongue, and released out of the mouth in word form.

In August of 1973, the Word of the Lord came unto me saying, "If men would believe Me, long prayers are not necessary. Just speaking the Word will bring what you desire. My creative power is given to man in Word form. I have ceased for a time from My work and have given man the book of MY CREATIVE POWER. That power is STILL IN MY WORD.

"For it to be effective, man must speak it in faith. Jesus spoke it when He was on earth, and as it worked then, so shall it work now. *But it must be spoken by the body.* Man must rise up and have dominion over the power of evil by My Words. It is My greatest desire that My people create a better life by the spoken Word. For My Word has not lost its power just because it has been spoken once. It is still equally as powerful today as when I said, 'Let there be light.'

"But for My Word to be effective, *men must speak it,* and that creative power will come forth performing that which is spoken in faith.

"My Word is not void of power.

"My people are void of speech. They hear the world and speak as the world speaks. By observing circumstances they have lost sight of My Word. They even speak that which the enemy says, and they destroy their own inheritance by corrupt communication of fear and unbelief.

"No Word of Mine is void of power, only powerless when it is unspoken.

"As there is creative power in My spoken Word, so is there evil power present in the words of the enemy to afflict and oppress everyone that speaks them.

"Be not conformed, but be transformed into the body of faith, knowing that My Words are alive evermore. Believe, speak, and obtain that your joy may be full and you shall be complete in Me." These truths changed my life. I have never been the same.

You will never be the same after learning the faith principles of Mark 11:23-24, Matthew 17:20, and Psalm 107:2. Your confession will come into line with the Word of God. You will have learned to release the ability of God within you by the spoken Word.

Confess victory in the face of apparent defeat. Confess abundance in the face of apparent lack.

Even as you read this, there may seem to be pressing needs. But — *my God is able and He will deliver you.* He will supply all your need according to His riches in glory by Christ Jesus (which is the Word of God).

In September of 1973, the Lord spoke to me concerning a teaching ministry.

He said, "Teach My people how to make My creative power work for them."

Then in June of 1974, I was teaching a faith seminar in Hickory, North Carolina. My text was taken from Mark 11:23. The Word of the Lord came unto me as I was teaching and spoke one of the most profound statements I have ever heard. It was simple, but then Jesus never made anything hard to understand. It is so simple that it almost seems foolish, but it has changed many lives.

It will change yours as you receive it. Let's put it in the context of which He spoke. Mark 11:23, "For verily I say unto you, That whosoever shall say unto this mountain, Be thou removed, and be thou cast into the sea; and shall not doubt in his heart, but shall believe that those things which he saith shall come to pass; he shall have whatsoever he saith."

As I was teaching from this text, Jesus said to me, "I have told my people they can have WHAT THEY SAY and they are SAYING WHAT THEY HAVE."

That is a very simple truth, but oh how profound and far reaching. For as long as you say what you have, you will have what you say, then you again say what you have, and it will produce no more than what you say.

You can see that you have set a spiritual law in motion that will confine you to the very position or circumstance you are in when you set that law in motion. It is an age-old problem of not looking beyond what you can see with the physical eye.

The things that are seen are temporal. "While we look not at the things which are seen, but at the things which are not seen: for the things which are seen are temporal; but the things which are not seen are eternal" (2 Cor. 4:18). The word *"temporal"* means subject to change. The circumstances of life, your position in life, the problems you face in life are very real to you because you see them, feel them, and hear them, but thank God, the very fact that you can see and touch them means they are subject to change.

A correct application of this spiritual law will change even the most impossible situation. But, to incorrectly apply these laws will hold you in bondage and cause the circumstance to grow worse.

Every faith principle, every spiritual law that God set forth in His Word was for your benefit. It was designed to put you over in life. It was not designed to hold you back or put you in bondage. But just as Satan has perverted nature to cause storms, floods, and destruction, so has he set out to pervert the law of God (Word of God) in the minds and hearts of God's people to the point where it looks as though God is the author of poverty, sickness, and the problems of life.

The truth is, in so many cases, the deception of Satan has caused an incorrect application of certain spiritual laws that defeat so many at the game of life.

GOD'S WORD IS SPIRITUAL LAW

God's Word always works, but the same law can work for or against you, depending on how you apply it.

So many times people will start confessing that they will not have enough money to make the payments on their house three months before they are due. They confess lack and the inability to obtain the money several times a day until the day finally arrives. Then they proudly announce through tears of self-pity, "See, I told you we couldn't make the payments. We never have enough money to go around. I can't understand why the people next door prosper in their wickedness."

If you were to listen to the wicked people next door, you would hear a different confession. Daily they confess and believe in prosperity, they talk prosperity, they live it. Wicked, yes, but they believe that they will prosper. They build a faith image inside themselves by the words they speak.

Many Christians who hear them think that they are just bragging, when they simply believed in prosperity and practice it.

Jesus Himself said the children of the world are wiser than the children of the kingdom. Wicked — yes, but God is no respecter of persons. They have learned the power of words. Many of them don't know what makes it work, they just know it works, and they practice it (spiritual law).

LEARN TO RELEASE YOUR FAITH IN WORDS

You can have what you say if you learn to release faith from the heart in your words.

Jesus said, **"...as thou hast believed, so be it done unto thee..."** (Matt. 8:13). He didn't say it would only work if you believed right. Whether you believe right or wrong, it is still the law. **"...God is not mocked: for whatsoever a man soweth that shall he also reap"** (Gal. 6:7).

The spiritual law is based on the same basic principle of seedtime and harvest. The words you speak are seeds that produce after their kind. Just as sure as they are planted, you can be equally sure a harvest will follow.

FAITH AS A SEED

"And the apostles said unto the Lord, Increase our faith. And the Lord said, If ye had faith as a grain of mustard seed, ye might say unto this sycamine tree, Be thou plucked up by the root, and be thou planted in the sea; and it should obey you" (Luke 17:5,6). We find in the above scripture that Jesus spoke of a seed that was so full of faith that it would speak. The apostles had asked Him to give them more faith. Jesus didn't indicate they needed more faith. In so many words, He said, "You don't need more faith, you need to sow the seed you already have."

Jesus told two great secrets in verse 6. Number one, *Faith is a seed*. Number two, The way you *plant a seed of faith* is to *say it*.

Faith talks. When faith talks, it talks faith, not fear *and unbelief*.

Jesus said your faith would speak to the object (sycamine tree), and it should obey *you*. In other words, the object would be obedient to *your* words. IT should obey *you*.

Now, let's bring this into focus. IT (poverty) should obey you. You said, "We don't ever have enough money. We will never be able to meet the payments"; and IT (poverty) followed you home. You sneezed and said, "I am taking a cold." AND IT (the cold) was obedient to your words and the virus fastened itself to your body. You said, "I just can't remember anything anymore." IT (your memory) became obedient to your words. You said, "My nerves are on edge." IT (your nervous system) became obedient, because Jesus said, IT SHOULD OBEY YOU.

Then again, we hear the words of Jesus, "If ye have faith as a grain of mustard seed, you shall say to this mountain, Remove hence to yonder place and IT SHALL REMOVE and NOTHING SHALL BE IMPOSSIBLE TO YOU" (Matt. 17:20).

Jesus did not say God would move the mountain.

That mustard seed has faith in the ability that resides on the inside of it, not in the hull that surrounds it. Jesus said, IF you have faith in the ability of Him that is inside you, you *SHALL SAY, REMOVE*, and IT (mountain, object) *SHALL REMOVE.*

FAITH IS THE VOICE OF AUTHORITY

These things know the voice of authority.

YOUR FAITH IS YOUR VOICE OF AUTHORITY.
Be careful what you authorize things to do.

Jesus said you can have what you say, and many have prophesied defeat, month after month, until the harvest time finally came, and it was true to the law of Genesis. *Defeat, lack, and inability were harvested in abundance.* **"For by thy words thou shalt be justified, and by thy words thou shalt be condemned"** *(Matt. 12:37).*

I know a family who planned a trip abroad. But, several weeks before they were to leave, the lady began to sow seed by the words of her mouth. She told several people on different occasions, *"I know exactly what will happen. The day we are to leave my kids will come down sick."* The very day they were to leave, the harvest came. Her boy was sick. She was heard to proclaim very proudly, *"I knew it would happen. I have said all along, the day we were to leave my kids will get sick."* The fruit of her mouth had won out again, but she was rather pleased that she had been able to prophesy it several weeks in advance.

"A man shall be satisfied with good by the fruit of his mouth: and the recompence of a man's hands shall be rendered unto him" (Prov. 12:14). "He shutteth his eyes to devise froward things: moving his lips he bringeth evil to pass" (Prov. 16:30).

The words of Jesus somehow seem to fit here. "A good man out of the good treasure of the heart bringeth forth good things: and an evil man out of the evil treasure bringeth forth evil things" (Matt. 12:35). *Notice who brought them forth (man, not God).*

THE TREASURES OF THE HEART CANNOT BE HIDDEN, BUT ARE MANIFEST THROUGH WORDS

Learn to take the Words of Jesus personally.

In Mark 11:23, Jesus tells you that you can have what you say if what you say comes from faith in your heart.

What would happen if Jesus walked down the aisles of your church, laid His hands on the people, and said, "It will come to pass that after I have laid my hand on each one of you, everything you say will happen just as you say it"?

Half of the congregation would jump up and say, "That just *tickles me to death!*" And you would be two weeks burying the dead.

The enemy has so programmed the minds of people until instead of resisting him, they have just sort of buddied up with him and begun to talk his language.

TRAIN YOURSELF
TO SPEAK GOD'S WORD

Let us train ourselves to speak God's Word. Ephesians 5:1 tells us, **"Be ye therefore followers of God, as dear children."** The word "followers" in the Greek means to imitate. We *are to imitate God as a child does his father.* If a child imitates his father, he will walk like him, talk like him, and pattern his every move after him.

We should not do less after our Father, God.

Jesus said He did that which He saw His Father do (John 5:19). He said His Father had given Him a commandment (what He should speak). Let's read it out of the Amplified Version of the Bible, John 12:47-50, **"If any one hears My teachings and fails to observe them — does not keep them, but disregards them — it is not I who judges him. For I have not come to judge and to condemn and to pass sentence and to inflict penalty on** the world, but to save the world. Any one who rejects Me and persistently sets Me at naught, *refusing* to accept My *teachings*, has his judge (however); for the (very) *messag*e that I have spoken will *itself* judge and convict him on the last day. This is because I have never spoken on My own authority or of My own accord or self-appointed, but the Father Who has sent Me has Himself given Me orders what to say and what to tell. *(Deut. 18:18,19)*. And I know that His commandment is (means,) eternal life. So whatever I speak, I am saying (exactly) what My Father has told Me to say and in accordance with *His instructions.*"

I'll paraphrase the above scripture. Jesus said, "The Father gave me instructions. What I should say, and those Words spoken, would produce life, and whatever I speak is exactly what the Father said."

When you study the life of Jesus you find several important facts that caused Him to overcome the world, the flesh, and the devil. I will list a few.

1. He spent much time in prayer, but He never prayed the problem, He prayed the answer — *what*

God said is the answer.

2. He spoke accurately, never crooked speech. His conversation always consisted of what God said.

3. He always spoke the end results, *not the problem.* Never did He confess present circumstances. He spoke the *desired results.*

4. He used the written Word to defeat Satan. For example, Matthew 4:3,4,10,11, "And when the tempter came to him, he said, If thou be the Son of God, command that these stones be made bread. ...It is written, Man shall not live by bread alone. ...Then saith Jesus unto him, Get thee hence, Satan: for it is written, Thou shalt worship the Lord thy God, and him only shalt thou serve. Then the devil leaveth him, and, behold, the angels came and ministered unto him." Satan left only after Jesus said, "Get thee hence."

5. Jesus always spoke directly to the problem, such as trees, storms, waves, demons, and Satan, and they all obeyed Him. Contrary to what most of us have thought, they did not obey Jesus because He

was the Son of God, but because He was the Son of man. John 5:26-27 tells us, **"For as the Father hath life in himself; so hath he given to the Son to have life in himself; And hath given him authority to execute judgment also, because he is the Son of man."** Not because He was the Son of God, but "BECAUSE HE IS THE SON OF MAN." He operated as a man on the authority of His Father's Word.

People who are born on this earth are the only ones who have authority here.

That is why God works through men.

Jesus knew how to operate in the authority of God's Word. It stands out very vividly in Matthew 4:10-11, "...Get thee hence, Satan: for it is written...Then the devil leaveth him."

He (the devil) will leave you as quickly as he did Jesus when you speak boldly the written Word.

THE WORD OF GOD CONCEIVED IN THE HEART, FORMED BY THE TONGUE, AND

SPOKEN OUT OF THE MOUTH IS CREATIVE POWER.

The spoken Word will work for you as you continually confess it.

CHAPTER 10

GOD'S WORD IS MEDICINE

(As given to me by the Great Physician)

Proverbs 4:20-22 says, "...attend to my words...they are life...and health (medicine) to all their flesh."

God's Word ministers to the total man. His Word (Jesus) is our wisdom, righteousness, sanctification, and redemption.

Most people have used the words of their mouth to hold themselves in bondage. But as you begin to speak the Word of God from the heart, it will produce liberty. It will produce the health and healing the Word said it would.

Most people have spoken contrary to the Word. They have spoken things that the devil has said. They have quoted what the enemy has said about them. Therefore, they have established on earth the words the enemy has said.

If we will begin to establish the things God said and establish His Word on this earth, then thank God, we'll rise to a new level of faith. We will walk in the level of life where we release the ability of God by the words of our mouth. We can release the ability of God within ourselves by the words of our mouth and cause His Word and His power to become available in us.

Let's learn to take God's medicine daily.

GOS-PILL
CAPPS-SULES

TO DEFEAT WORRY AND FEAR
CONFESS THESE GOS-PILLS
THREE TIMES A DAY

*No Harmful Side Effects

"I am the body of Christ and Satan hath no power over me. For I overcome evil with good" (1 Cor. 12:27; Rom. 12:21).

"I am of God and have overcome him (Satan). For greater is He that is in me, than he that is in the world" (1 John 4:4).

"I will fear no evil for thou art with me Lord, your Word and your Spirit they comfort me" (Ps. 23:4).

"I am far from oppression, and fear does not come nigh me" (Isa. 54:14).

"No weapon formed against me shall prosper, for my righteousness is of the Lord. But whatever I do will prosper for I'm like a tree that's planted by the rivers of water" (Isa. 54:17; Ps. 1:3).

"I am delivered from the evils of this present world for it is the will of God..." (Gal. 1:4).

"No evil will befall me neither shall any plague come nigh my dwelling. For you have given your angels charge over me and they keep me in all my ways, and in my pathway is life and there is no death" (Ps. 91:10,11; Prov. 12:28).

"I am a doer of the Word of God and am blessed in my deeds. I am happy in those things which I do because I am a doer of the Word of God" (James 1:22).

"I take the shield of faith and I quench every fiery dart that the wicked one brings against me" (Eph. 6:16).

"Christ has redeemed me from the curse of the law. Therefore, I forbid any sickness or disease to come upon this body. Every disease germ and every virus that touches this body dies instantly in the Name of Jesus. Every organ and every tissue of this body functions in the perfection to which God created it to function, and I forbid any malfunction in this body, in the Name of Jesus" (Gal. 3:13; Rom. 8:11; Gen. 1:30; Matt. 16:19).

"I am an overcomer and I overcome by the blood of the Lamb and the word of my testimony" (Rev. 12:11).

"The devil flees from me because I resist him in the Name of Jesus" (James 4:7).

"The Word of God is forever settled in heaven. Therefore, I establish His Word upon this earth" (Ps. 119:89).

"Great is the peace of my children for they are taught of the Lord" (Isa. 54:13).

FOR MATERIAL NEEDS CONFESS THESE THREE TIMES A DAY

"Christ has redeemed me from the curse of the law. Christ has redeemed me from poverty, Christ has redeemed me from sickness, Christ has redeemed me from spiritual death" (Gal. 3:13; Deut. 28).

"For poverty He has given me wealth, for sickness He has given me health, for death He has given me eternal life" (2 Cor. 8:9; John 10:10; John 5:24).

"It is true unto me according to the Word of God" (Ps. 119:25).

"I delight myself in the Lord and He gives me the desires of my heart" (Ps. 37:4).

"I have given and it is given unto me good measure, pressed down, shaken together, running over, men given unto my bosom" (Luke 6:38).

"With what measure I mete, it is measured unto me. I sow bountifully, therefore I reap bountifully. I give cheerfully, and my God has made all grace abound toward me and I having all sufficiency of all things do abound to all good works" (2 Cor. 9:6-8).

"There is no lack for my God supplieth all of my need according to His riches in glory by Christ Jesus" (Phil. 4:19).

"The Lord is my shepherd and I DO NOT WANT because Jesus was made poor that I through His poverty might have abundance. For He came that I might have life and have it more abundantly" (Ps. 23:1; 2 Cor. 8:9; John 10:10).

"And I, having received the gift of righteousness do reign as a king in life by Jesus Christ" (Rom. 5:17).

"The Lord has pleasure in the prosperity of His servant, and Abraham's blessings are mine" (Ps. 35:27; Gal. 3:14).

FOR WISDOM AND GUIDANCE CONFESS THESE THREE TIMES A DAY

"The Spirit of truth abideth in me and teaches me all things and He guides me into all truths. Therefore I confess I have perfect knowledge of every situation and every circumstance that I come up against. For I have the wisdom of God" (John 16:13; James 1:5).

"I trust in the Lord with all of my heart, and I lean not unto my own understanding" (Prov. 3:5).

"In all my ways I acknowledge Him and He directs my path" (Prov. 3:6).

"The Word of God is a lamp unto my feet, it is a light unto my path" (Ps. 119:105).

"The Lord will perfect that which concerneth me" (Ps. 138:8).

"I let the Word of Christ dwell in me richly in all wisdom" (Col. 3:16).

"I do follow the good shepherd and I know His voice and the voice of a stranger I will not follow" (John 10:4,5).

"Jesus is made unto me wisdom, righteousness, sanctification, and redemption. Therefore I confess I have the wisdom of God, and I am the righteousness of God in Christ Jesus" (1 Cor. 1:30; 2 Cor. 5:21).

"I am filled with the knowledge of the Lord's will in all wisdom and spiritual understanding" (Col. 1:9).

"I am a new creation in Christ, I am His workmanship created in Christ Jesus. Therefore I have the mind of Christ and the wisdom of God is formed within me" (2 Cor. 5:17; Eph. 2:10; 1 Cor. 2:16).

"I have put off the old man and have put on the new man, which is renewed in the knowledge after the image of Him that created me" (Col. 3:10).

"I receive the Spirit of wisdom and revelation in the knowledge of Him, the eyes of my understanding being enlightened. And I am not conformed to this world but I am transformed by the renewing of my mind. My mind is renewed by the Word of God" (Eph. 1:17,18; Rom. 12:2).

FOR COMFORT AND STRENGTH CONFESS THESE AS OFTEN AS NECESSARY

"I am increasing in the knowledge of God. I am strengthened with all might according to His glorious power" (Col. 1:10,11).

"I am delivered from the power of darkness and I am translated into the kingdom of His dear Son" (Col.1:13).

"I am born of God and I have world overcoming faith residing on the inside of me. For greater is He that is in me, than he that is in the world" (1 John 5:4,5; 1 John 4:4).

"I will do all things through Christ which strengtheneth me" (Phil. 4:13).

"The joy of the Lord is my strength. The Lord is the strength of my life" (Neh. 8:10; Ps. 27:1).

"The peace of God which passeth all understanding keeps my heart and my mind through Christ Jesus. And all things which are good, and pure, and perfect, and lovely, and of good report, I think on these things" (Phil. 4:7,8).

"I speak the truth of the Word of God in love and I grow up into the Lord Jesus Christ in all things" (Eph. 4:15).

"I let no corrupt communication proceed out of my mouth, but that which is good to edifying, that it may minister grace to the hearer. I grieve not the Holy Spirit of God, whereby I'm sealed unto the day of redemption" (Eph. 4:29,30).

"No man shall take me out of his hand for I have eternal life" (John 10:29).

"I let the peace of God rule in my heart and I refuse to worry about anything" (Col. 3:15).

"I will not let the Word of God depart from before my eyes for it is life to me for I have found it and it is health and healing to all my flesh" (Prov. 4:21,22).

"God is on my side. God is in me now, who can be against me? He has given unto me all things that pertain unto life and godliness. Therefore I am a partaker of His divine nature" (2 Cor. 6:16; John 10:10; 2 Peter 1:3,4; Rom. 8:31).

"I am a believer and these signs do follow me. In the Name of Jesus I cast out demons, I speak with new tongues, I lay hands on the sick and they do recover" (Mark 16:17,18).

"Jesus gave me the authority to use His name. And that which I bind on earth is bound in heaven. And that which I loose on earth is loosed in heaven. Therefore in the Name of the Lord Jesus Christ I bind the principalities, the powers, the rulers of the darkness of this world. I bind and cast down spiritual wickedness in high places and render them harmless and ineffective against me in the Name of Jesus" (Matt. 16:19; Matt. 18:18; Eph. 6:12).

"I am complete in Him who is the head of all principality and power. For I am His workmanship, created in Christ Jesus unto good works which God has before ordained that I should walk therein" (Col. 2:10; Eph. 2:10).

God created the universe by the methods which you have just put into motion by the words of your mouth. God released His faith in words. Man is created in the image of God; therefore, man releases his faith in words. Words are the most powerful things in the universe today.

Let me say it again, "The Word of God conceived in the human spirit, formed by the tongue, and spoken out of the mouth becomes creative power that will work for you."

If the body of Christ would only grasp the truths and the principles that are taught in this book and put them in action, they would change this world in twenty-four hours.

Jesus said, "I HAVE TOLD MY PEOPLE THEY CAN HAVE WHAT THEY SAY, BUT MY PEOPLE ARE SAYING WHAT THEY HAVE."

WORDS ARE THE MOST POWERFUL THINGS IN THE UNIVERSE

The words you speak will either put you over in life or hold you in bondage. Many people have been held captive in their circumstances by their own words. The absence of

God's Word in your life will rob you of faith in His ability.

RECEIVE FROM GOD

Put yourself in a position to receive God's best for you by speaking His Word. God's Creative Power® is still just as it was in the beginning of time, when He stood there and said, "Light — be," and light was. His Word spoken from your mouth and conceived in your heart becomes a spiritual force releasing His ability within you.

CREATIVE POWER IN YOU

Man was created in the image of God and His likeness. Learn to speak His faith-filled words to your situation and see your life transformed. Allow God's Creative Power® to flow from you.

I have told my people they can have what they say, but my people are saying what they have.

PRAYER OF SALVATION

od loves you—no matter who you are, no matter what your past. God loves you so much that He gave His one and only begotten Son for you. The Bible tells us that "...whoever believes in him shall not perish but have eternal life" (John 3:16 New International Version). Jesus laid down His life and rose again so that we could spend eternity with Him in heaven and experience His absolute best on earth. If you would like to receive Jesus into your life, pray the following prayer out loud and mean it from your heart.

> *Heavenly Father, I come to You admitting that I am a sinner. Right now, I choose to turn away from sin, and I ask You to cleanse me of all unrighteousness. I believe that Your Son, Jesus, died on the cross to take away my*

sins. I also believe that He rose again from the dead so that I might be forgiven of my sins and made righteous through faith in Him. I call upon the Name of Jesus Christ and confess Him to be the Savior and Lord of my life. Jesus, I choose to follow You and ask that You fill me with the power of the Holy Spirit. I declare that right now I am a child of God. I am free from sin and full of the righteousness of God. I am saved in Jesus' name. Amen.

ABOUT
THE AUTHORS

Charles Capps a farmer from England, Arkansas, became an internationally known Bible teacher by sharing practical truths from the Word of God. His simplistic, down-to-earth style of applying spiritual principles to daily life has appealed to people from every Christian denomination.

The requests for speaking engagements became so great after the printing of *God's Creative Power® Will Work for You* that he retired from farming and became a full-time Bible teacher. His books are available in multiple languages throughout the world.

Besides publishing 24 books, including best-sellers *The Tongue: A Creative Force* and *God's Creative Power*® series which has sold over 7 million copies. Capps Ministries has a national daily radio broadcast and weekly TV broadcast called *Concepts of Faith.*

ABOUT
THE AUTHORS

Annette **Capps** is an ordained minister, business-woman and licensed airplane pilot. A lifelong student of the Bible, her curiosity led her to investigate the similarities of "quantum physics" and the teachings of Jesus Christ. This powerful combination opened new dimensions for those seeking a bridge between the Bible and modern science.

Building on her former teaching subjects such as *The Mind-Body Connection, Changing the Course of Your Life,* and *Realizing Your Dreams by Restoring Your Hope,* she demonstrates the practical application of spiritual principles in everyday life.

Guest appearances on the *Concepts of Faith* television program with her father, author & teacher, Charles Capps generated extraordinary interest as have radio interviews and magazine articles. In addition to the book, *Quantum Faith*®, Annette has authored five other books entitled; *Reverse the Curse in Your Body & Emotions*, *Removing the Roadblocks to Health & Healing*, *Overcoming Persecution*, *Angels* and *God's Creative Power*® *for Finances*.

Annette and her husband reside in Tulsa, Oklahoma, where she is the President of Capps Ministries which has locations in both Arkansas and Oklahoma.

For a complete list of CDs, DVDs, and books by Capps Ministries, write:

Capps Ministries

P.O. Box 10, Broken Arrow, Oklahoma 74013

Toll Free Order Line (24 hours)
1-877-396-9400

www.cappsministries.com

VISIT US ONLINE FOR:

Radio Broadcasts in Your Area

Concepts of Faith *Television Broadcast listings:*
Local Stations, **Daystar***,* **VICTORY** *&* **TCT**
Television Network

E-Books & MP3s Available

youtube.com/CappsMinistries

facebook.com/CharlesCappsMinistries

BOOKS BY CHARLES CAPPS

BOOKS BY CHARLES CAPPS AND ANNETTE CAPPS

Angels

God's Creative Power® for Finances
(Also available in Spanish)

God's Creative Power® – Gift Edition
(Also available in Spanish)

BOOKS BY ANNETTE CAPPS

Quantum Faith®
(Also available in Spanish)

Reverse the Curse in Your Body and Emotions

Removing the Roadblocks to Health and Healing

Overcoming Persecution

CALLING THINGS THAT ARE NOT

The Powerful Realm of the Unseen

The principle of calling things that are not as though they were is the spiritual principle through which everything physical becomes manifest. God created light by calling for "light" when only darkness was there. Jesus used this same method, call the lepers clean, and the dead to life, and peace to the storm.

You must call for what you desire. If you want your dog to come, you call the dog. You call for what is not there. Whatever you call in the natural will come. Call what does not exist and continue to call until it manifests.

ISBN 13: 978-1-937578-31-2

Removing the Roadblocks to Health and Healing

In order to receive healing and live in health, you must prayerfully evaluate your life as a whole and allow the Holy Spirit to guide you into wellness.

In this book, Annette Capps gives a insightful, practical look at the emotional and spiritual hindrances that believers face daily.

Recognizing and removing these roadblocks can enable you to receive healing and walk in health and wholeness.

- claiming sickness as belonging to you
- belief in tribal DNA
- using infirmity as a tool
- holding on to negative emotions
- refusing to forgive
- feeding the spirit of infirmity
- ignoring the leadings of the Holy Spirit and your spirit
- staying in an unhealthy environment
- trying to act beyond your faith
- believing you will be healed in the future

ISBN 13: 978-1-937578-58-9

Seedtime and Harvest

God's Word is incorruptible seed, and God's promises are seeds for harvest. In this book you will learn that as you speak God's promises out of your mouth as a seed, it goes into your heart to grow and produce a harvest of blessing.

ISBN-13: 978-0-9819574-3-2

The Thermostat of Hope

Surely no one would be foolish enough in natural things to argue with you when you turn the thermostat to 70 degrees, but they will when you set your goal on God's promises.

Hope, like a thermostat, is simply a goal-setter with no substance. Faith, which comes from the heart, is the substance of what you desire.

The heart (spirit) of man is like the heart of the heating-cooling unit. Designed by God to produce the very thing you plant in it. You plant it or set the goal by speaking it!

ISBN-13: 978-1-937578-30-5

The Harrison House Vision

Proclaiming the truth and the power

of the Gospel of Jesus Christ with excellence.

Challenging Christians

to live victoriously,

grow spiritually,

know God intimately.

Connect with us on

f Facebook @ HarrisonHousePublishers

and ◙ Instagram @ HarrisonHousePublishing

so you can stay up to date with news

about our books and our authors.

Visit us at **www.harrisonhouse.com**

for a complete product listing as well as

monthly specials for wholesale distribution.

Fast. Easy.
Convenient.

For the latest Harrison House product information and author news, look no further than your computer. All the details on our powerful, life-changing products are just a click away. New releases, email subscriptions, testimonies, monthly specials—find them all in one place. Visit harrisonhouse.com today!